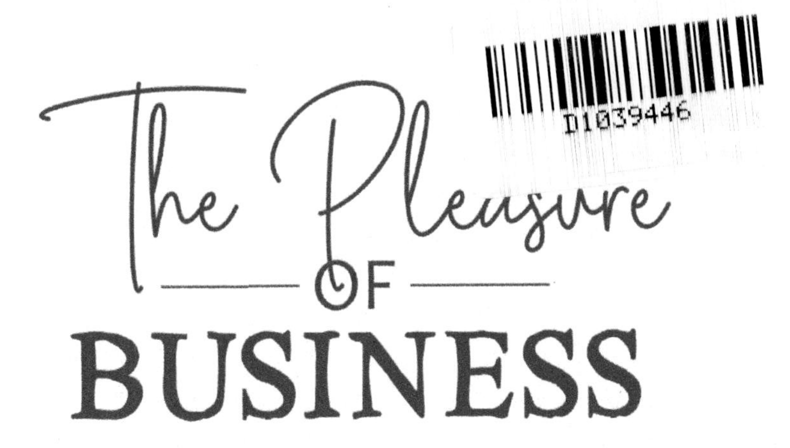


PRINCIPLES AND GUIDELINES HOW TO BUILD, BALANCE, AND BENEFIT FROM ANY RELATIONSHIP

DARNELL MEADOWS SR

# TABLE OF CONTENTS

# ACKNOWLEDGEMENT

Everyday above ground is a great day, I love and cherish my family without you all my world would be nothing, thank you to my Mother because without you choosing to take the responsibility to have me and be strong enough to raise a child on your own I wouldn't be here, you instilled king values in me and taught me to fear nothing. My beautiful grandmother for all of the unequivocal support. Arthur Frazier (pops) for teaching me the importance of hard work. Thank you to my sister and all my brother s, aunts, uncles, friends, and Extended family members. Most of all I love and appreciate my best friend Căoméi.

For being by my side every step of the way and to all of my children Dj, Dashiah ,Danaye , Camryn, journee, Aubrey I thank the most high for you because y'all give me the motivation to go harder ,do more , be more and help me to be a better individual every day I love you all and dedicate this book to you.

# FOREWORD

By Nicole Phillip

The power of entrepreneurship is undeniable. It's the force that drives innovation, new ideas, and economic development. It has been said by many prominent individuals that entrepreneurship is more difficult than any other profession because it involves so many different skill sets and disciplines.

Entrepreneurship is the way of the future! Finding success in a traditional job may no longer be an option. Entrepreneurship can give you what you've been looking for all along: personal freedom and ownership over your achievements. The process isn't easy, but it's worth every bit of effort if building empires really means something to you.

And if you're willing to put forth all those necessary efforts: entrepreneurship might just be what it takes!

As an entrepreneur for over 16 years, I have seen the light go out of many people's eyes and watched as they crumbled under the weight of entrepreneurship. I know all too well what it feels like when you just want to throw your hands up and quit--it is very easy. I remember the fear that overwhelmed me as I was laid off from my corporate job. The security I thought I had was gone in a blink of an eye. But it catapulted into full-time entrepreneurship.

In today's economy, there is a lot of talk about the importance of entrepreneurship. It seems like everywhere you turn, someone has an opinion on whether or not starting your own business is the way to go. But what does it really take to be a successful entrepreneur? How can you make sure that your company will succeed in this cutthroat market? In this blog post I am going to outline five key traits of entrepreneurs and their companies which will help them stay afloat in these tough economic times. Let's get started!

Success isn't complicated: there are two ingredients needed—focus on daily action (or progress) with consistency over an extended period of time without quitting out on oneself during tough times, then following up with appropriate.

When you find something you're passionate about, success is inevitable. Success does not happen overnight but instead happens by taking one step at a time- and that's how it should be! As they say "nothing worth having comes easy" so the work never stops until your dreams of success become reality. Don't wait for somebody else to create the life you want because this will only lead to disappointment; take control today and make what matters most in life come true through achieving great goals each day no matter how big or small!

But for Darnell, it's always been worth every ounce to pursue his passion and live a life without regret. He is a successful go-getter with tenacity and grit. I've seen him fight through almost losing his company to building back up to a seven-figure business again. He's made many mistakes and learned from them, but he never gave up on himself or his team. His favorite thing in the world is seeing people grow into their potential and become better versions of themselves, whether it be as an entrepreneur or just a person in general. He may not had always had the smoothest path, but he seized the opportunities that came his way.

Every entrepreneur has a story. Some are successes, some failures, but the most interesting stories are those that contain both. I've been fortunate to be able to work with Darnell over my career and have learned a lot from him about what it takes to build a successful business.

In this book, Darnell shares his mistakes and growth as an entrepreneur. He's had ups and downs in his industry, but when he talks about his failures, it's obvious that he learned something valuable from them. He shares some insights on how he made it through difficult times. Darnell doesn't let anything get in the way of success - whether that be people or even himself!

The struggles of an entrepreneur are immense. It's hard to be an entrepreneur. You have to be a jack of all trades, and you're always on call. From the constant pressure to be innovative and creative, to the lack of financial stability that comes with self-employment, entrepreneurs have a tough road ahead. But for those who can persevere through these challenges, there is a great reward on the other side.

There are many joys that come with it too: the thrill of creating something new, watching your idea grow and evolve as you learn more about what people want from your product or service. It can make even the most stressful moments seem like they were worth it in the end because of how much joy comes with being an entrepreneur. The chapters will explore some of those joys in more detail so you know what to expect before taking the leap into entrepreneurship yourself!

For many people who want to start their own business or pursue entrepreneurship as a side hustle while they work another job, fear may hold you back from taking that leap into full-time entrepreneurship. However, if you're looking for some honest advice from someone who has been there before and made it out alive then listen up: You don't need much more than passion and perseverance in order to make your dream happen!

Because you're reading this book, I know you're interested in starting your own business or are already in the process of doing so, this book will teach you everything about the pleasures and pain of a boss. The struggle of being an entrepreneur is real. It's hard to keep up with the demands of running a business and it can be lonely going at it alone. However, you're not alone. Darnell outlines key traits of entrepreneurs and their companies which will help them stay afloat in these tough economic times.

# CHAPTER 1

# SEED OF SIGNIFICANCE

The truth only means something if the person who's listening understands it. With that said, I hope and pray you get true clarity and understanding from this book.

People often asked me, "When did you realize you wanted to be an entrepreneur?"

I've always heard that entrepreneurship was a calling. It's a lifestyle that many people know they want to lead before they're even in a position to do so. I consider myself an entrepreneur, but I came to that realization after years of walking side by side with hustlers. Personally, this journey of business has been a long, hard, yet pleasurable one. People often say you should not mix business and pleasure. Well, I never had that mindset. I love the pleasure of doing business.

My first introduction to a business mindset was in the late 80's early 90's.

Dezz, short for Desmond, happens to be one of my closest family members growing up. He had it rough as he faced some difficult times during his childhood. He was a boy who grew up in the ghetto & the one who meets all the trials & tribulations of a cruel world. He was forced to grow up as he learned survival at the early age of 5. I could go on and on, but his life taught me so much about meeting needs which is the backbone of entrepreneurship.

He may not know this, but he gave me the first introduction to marketing and customer service. We would sneak off and go to the local supermarket when we stayed in the projects Cleveland Arms in Duval County, Jacksonville, Fl. We would ask people if they needed help with their groceries and would help them to the car and load up the groceries for a tip. What I learned, even though I did not know it at the time, was the concept of 'meritocracy, which means "what you earn is directly correlated to how much effort you put in. This was genius!

I laugh to myself now that I think of it. Did we help the grocery stores meet their needs, such as implementing better protocol and customer service?

When you look at the tag that the baggers wear, maybe the next time you're at Publix, it says to "carry out services is our pleasure please no tipping" in bold letters. That makes me smile and think back to being 5 or 6 years old, making $10 - 30 dollars in an hour. For me, it was a fun experience, but it was survival for Dezz.

Another lesson I learned at that time was **loyalty and the value of money.** I was an only child at the time, so I was highly blessed to have all the toys and necessities of life, so I mastered the act of sharing. When people work together to achieve the same goal or targets, they SHARE ideas, loyalty, and methods to complete their tasks. They share RESOURCES. **I learned to** take care of others. Often we have many things that others do not have. It's only right we share those things with them.

On the other hand, the money we made taught me how to invest and flip my money, and I learned how demand and supply worked. This was quite interesting for me. I began to sell items to my friends and neighbors based on what they seemed to want and need. We didn't have a penny store on our side of town, so I positioned myself to become a store. I would buy candy and cookies by the pack (dozens) for as low as 1 dollar for each package, and I would sell six cookies for 25cents which turned a dollar pack of cookies into $4.25. The candy was 5 cents each, so I made over 4x profit, a total of $40-$50 off of a $10-$12 investment.

I also ran errands for my grandma, and she would give me dollars as a reward. In a real sense, I wasn't spending my money to buy those goodies.

As time went by, I had three other kids working for me, and I would give them a percentage of the daily sales, which they would turn right around and spend it on the same snacks we were selling.

At the time, I didn't know I had created a complete business model and even created opportunities for others. I had a vision, and I was consistent in my work.

The harder I worked, the greater the rewards (money in this case), and the more I could live my life by my own rules and not have to ask my parents for money now and then. I believe that this was (and is) a pivotal point in my formative years where the "seeds of the **Entrepreneurial Spirit" were sown**. Those seeds, however, took many years to germinate before I began my first true entrepreneurial venture properly.

With my wealth of experience, I now teach people how to recognize a profitable business when they see one, avoid pitfalls in business and have the **courage, drive, and initiative** to seize an opportunity when it arises.

In this book, you will understand that success is a person. You will know why they say success is peace of mind, NOT just about the accumulation of wealth and power.

This book will open your eyes to the inner abilities and balance in a relationship. You will no longer see business as pain but pleasure.

# CHAPTER 2

# BE SURE TO MODEL THE BEST IMAGE OF YOURSELF

***It is hard to make a man miserable while he feels worthy of himself.*** *– Abraham Lincoln*

Isn't it funny? We often look at other people and wish we could swap places with them because they appear to be so flawless, while they look at us and think the same thing.

Because we are engulfed in quiet desperation, we suffer from low self-esteem, lack self-confidence, and lose hope in self-improvement.

It's time you stop thinking of yourselves as second-rate being. In this chapter we are going to familiarize ourselves with what self-image means and tips on how to put your best self-image forward anywhere you go.

In its most basic form, a self-image is an internalized mental picture/idea of yourself. Your general outlook on life, including your level of happiness and fulfillment, is influenced by how you think and feel about yourself. This is also based on your appearance, performance, and relationships.

A person's self-image is the mental picture of details such as height, weight, hair color, gender, and also of things that have been learned by that person about himself or herself from others. “What do you think people think about you?" Defines a person's self-image. What a person believes others think about them is directly related to what that person thinks about him or herself.

Your self-image is a collective representation of your assets and liabilities based on your perception of yourself. To put it another way, your self-image is how you perceive yourself in terms of your strengths and weaknesses.

The labels you give yourself to describe your qualities and characteristics often reveal these assets and liabilities. For example, you might say, "I am intelligent, therefore I can..." or I’m a loser, so I don't think I can...

These are a few of the many labels you may give yourself, as well as the inevitable conclusions you may reach, and these labels serve as the foundations of your belief systems.

Your self-image is not based on reality; in fact, it is far from it. In actuality, your self-image is based on your perception of reality, which is influenced by how you believe society and other people view you.

An individual's personal feelings and perspectives are the foundation of a healthy self-image. They are no longer swayed by other people's perceptions of them or societal expectations. Instead, they form their own opinions about the internalized mental image/idea of themselves. As a result, these individuals frequently have a more positive outlook on life and, as a result, more confidence in themselves and their abilities. Why? Because they have a better sense of control over their lives.

A person with a positive self-image recognizes and accepts their flaws. In fact, they are realistic and recognize and accept that they have personal flaws. However, no critical judgment is made here. They recognize who they are and how they are right now, and they make the best of what they have.

A positive self-image is, of course, based on a strong sense of self-worth. Both collaborate to help shape a healthy personality, which effectively lays the groundwork for a successful life.

*Let's take a look at a four-step process that will assist you in projecting your best self-image.*

## Explore Yourself

The first step to take is to explore who you are and what that means to you? This is a massive first step because without a proper understanding of who you are, you may never develop a clear and accurate picture of who you really are

Ask yourself:

- Who am I?
- How am I?
- What defines me?
- How do I see myself?
- How do people see me?
- Are they right or am I just misunderstood?
- Is this really who I am? Is that true?
- Is this the real me? Is there something else going on beneath the surface?

It's crucial that you keep asking these questions to dig deeper, deeper and deeper. It's similar to peeling the layers off an onion. The layers on the surface will reveal a hazy picture of who you are. However, as you peel off more layers and dig deeper, you begin to get a clearer picture/idea of yourself. This is why it's critical to question your point of view on a regular basis. Because your goal is to model your best self-image, you must get to the core of who you are without the need for all those extra layers.

## Take a Personal Inventory

List your positive qualities, goals, passions, and purpose in a personal inventory. ***Consider the following questions:***

- What positive qualities do I possess? I am... so I can...
- What do people have to say about these positive qualities?
- What are my goals?
- How to live meaningfully and purposefully?
- What does all this mean to me?
- Why is it important?

The goal of this step is to unlock all of the positive feelings you have about yourself; **to unlock all of the things you have going for you that will now help form a powerful personal impression of who you are today from a larger perspective.**

You removed unnecessary layers in the previous step to get to the core of yourself. In this step, you'll build layers on top of that core to create a complete and accurate picture/idea of yourself right now. And, of course, your self-image is built on the foundations of that image.

## Analyze Your Struggles

A healthy self-image is based on our own personal feelings and perspectives, as I mentioned earlier. To put it another way, how we think about ourselves, as well as the opinions and labels we create, are all important factors in developing a positive self-image.

A person with a healthy self-image and self-worth does not define themselves based on the opinions of others or their circumstances. Instead, they must rely on internal resources for this. As a result, taking personal control of our internal world is critical because it is the only thing that truly counts when it comes to developing a positive self-image.

Changing your language patterns in this manner will help you calm down and think more clearly and effectively. As a result, you'll be less likely to make negative assumptions about yourself or label yourself in a bad and unhealthy way

## Develop a realistic image of yourself

The final step is to develop a more accurate image of yourself that you can use to build your best self-image.

This self-perception must be based on all of the positive qualities and abilities you identified in Step 2 of this process. Take those positive traits and strengths and ask yourself one simple question: How would I like to be in the ideal world?

Take some time to think about this question thoroughly and honestly, and then respond as to how you would like to begin today. Of course, there is no one correct answer, but rather a variety of responses that contribute to the formation of your self-image. Yes, you still have flaws and issues with which you may be dealing.

Accept them as they are. They are currently a part of you. Over time, you can work on improving these areas. What matters is that you are truthful, genuine, authentic, and genuine. You are who you are, and you see yourself as you are, flaws and all.

It's all about you in the end when it comes to developing a positive self-image. It's all about how you, and only you, see yourself, without any outside influences. And it is above all else this image/idea of "you" that matters. You are in control here; you are the only one who can define how you see yourself, and that is ultimately what matters.

Finally, a positive self-image is based on strong foundations of self-worth. **Self-worth is all about how much you value yourself, regardless of what others may say and/or despite adversity.** Nothing can shake or phase you when you have a high sense of self-worth. Similarly, when you have a positive self-image, you don't rely on others to define who you are.

You and only you are the one who defines who you are. In every situation, you and only you create the impression you have of yourself. Yes, you are the one who molds and shapes who you are today and who you will become tomorrow.

# CHAPTER 3

# DON'T JUST GO GET THE HOUSE AND LOSE THE HOME

People say that money can buy anything and thus it makes the world go round, but nothing compares to family. The people we're related to, by blood and marriage, are expected to be our closest and most powerful allies, our most reliable sources of love and support.

Our first and strongest emotional memories are formed in our families, and they continue to appear there.

Yes, money matters!

Having enough money to feel safe and live a comfortable lifestyle is unquestionably beneficial, but it can't compare to having a close relationship with the people you care about. If you don't put in the extra work to earn money, you'll have a lower quality of life; however, if you pay too much attention to money, you'll lose time and connections with your family, which will damage your relationship with them.

Some people are more interested in having a good time, others in achieving a personal goal, and still others forming strong bonds with others. Some people intend to make money that they consider more important than their family, while others give the best of themselves to everyone else and leave the rest of them to their families.

Prioritizing money and attempting to impress people who don't deserve your time and attention will not necessarily improve your mood daily. The poll published in the Journal of Personality and Social Psychology shows that there is a connection between money and life satisfaction (happiness), but not a very strong link between money and positive feelings and enjoyment of life. This implies that family has a significant impact on our emotional well-being, whereas money has only a minimal effect.

People who are liked and respected by others and those who believe they have some control over their circumstances are happier. Of course, money can make having this kind of control over your situation easier, but not enough to put it above happy family life.

Of course, money can make having this kind of control over your situation easier, but not enough to put it above happy family life.

## Materialism, Money, and Marriage

An excessive focus on money and material possessions is linked to depression and anxiety. Materialistic people are also more likely to make poor financial decisions, such as purchasing luxury items on credit. Married couples who placed a higher value on their relationship than on their finances were happier and more financially responsible. Whether your goal is to have more fulfilling relationships or to have more financial security, research suggests that prioritizing family over money is the way to go.

Remember, in pursuing business goals, we strive to survive and earn money for ourselves and our families. We fight for them, giving them everything you have and ensuring their future security. As a result, we can say no matter how much we achieve; it will be naught if "you get the house and lose our home."

Money is valuable, but we only value it because we require it to support our families. Some things cannot be purchased with, such as our family, which we may lose if we take them for granted. Let us not wait until then. Money will be useless in any case if we do not have our family to spend it with. You can't buy happiness with money, but you can get it from your family without paying for it.

# CHAPTER 4

# SUCCESS IS NOTHING WITHOUT SIGNIFICANCE

While many people measure their Success by wealth, recognition, power, and status, there's nothing wrong with those, but if that's all you're focused on, you're missing the boat. If you focus on significance -using your time and talent to serve others - that's when significant Success can come your way.

Many people either associate Success with significance, or they are so focused on achieving Success that they are willfully blind to the meaning of significance. With their wealth and professional accomplishments, this set of people will not achieve true greatness that only comes by making significant contributions to something other than themselves.

Most of these people use their knowledge, resources, and experience to acquire things to satisfy their personal goals and desires, which in their minds defines Success. This is unlike those that use their knowledge, resources, and experience to serve and benefit others, which by my standards constitutes significance.

## What makes Success any different from significance?

Success is about you. Success is based on what you achieve for yourself. Significance has to do with others. It is impossible to live a life of significance without helping others.

Success is about making a positive impact here and now, primarily by what you do and what you accomplish.

Significance is about a lasting impression of who you are and the edifying presence you bring to others.

Even though Success could be a powerful motivator and controls the lives of many, it is nothing without significance. Success comes to an end. Significance, on the other hand, will always outlast you. Your significance will still be yours even if you are no longer present. Nothing will ever take that from you.

Unlike Success, significance is a gift that keeps on giving. When you impact the life of another human being... and that person impacts the life of another... who in turn influences another.

The differences between sending your kids to a good school and **educating others is** what defines significance. Secondly, saving and retiring happy compared to **empowering others** with employment and a livelihood other than just your kids.

Strive to live a significant life rather than a successful one. However, you can eat your cake and have it. As you pursue significance, Success may come along also, but it shouldn't be your priority.

Quoting Zig Ziglar's famous principle, "You can have everything in life you want if you will help other people get what they want. Pouring ourselves into others should be our priority.

# CHAPTER 5

# MONEY IS NOTHING IF YOU HAVE NO MEANING

Money needs a purpose, but many of us, unfortunately, have grown accustomed to instant gratification. We see whatever we want and buy it.

We all have a limited amount fund, so we must ensure that whatever amount of discretionary money we have are spent on things we want. I want a lot of things, but not all of them at the same time. Some things are crucial to me, such as making memories with my family when we travel, while others, such as the nice outfit I saw at the department store, are far less so. If I don't have a purpose for my money, it's easy to fall prey to the allure of instant gratification and mindless spending, ending up with a lot of stuff but nothing that truly matters.

There is a purpose attached to having money and growing your finances. But what money can't do is **create meaning, otherwise known as purpose** in and of itself.

Consider yourself as a person living in a tent on an open plain. You decide to plant a tree one day. You are responsible for watering it for the next 40 years. You keep it safe from the elements and animals, but its fruit is never picked. It's not something you do for fun. You don't stop to rest in its shady nook. To build a house, you don't even fathom to cut down some branches. Because you're solely focused on growing that tree bigger and bigger, you never go anywhere or do anything else.

The tree eventually stops growing one day, shortly after your 70th birthday. You look up at its massive trunk and tangle of branches and think to yourself...

**What was that for?**

Many of us similarly treat our financial planning the same way. We become so engrossed in the process of "growing the tree" that we forget to think about harvesting the apples or timber to improve our lives. We'll keep working to grow our tree as long as it keeps growing, even if it doesn't involve our interests or use our unique talents to their highest potential.

Then there's the matter of retirement. Some soon-to-be retirees are lost when faced with the prospect of no longer working. They never stopped considering what that next dollar was really for because their sense of purpose was so entwined with working hard to make more money.

A motivational speaker and life coach asked a question in a gathering of young folks. Her question was, what do you want in life?" and a young girl answering saying she wants a million dollars. She then asked her why she wanted a million dollars. The young girl said, "I want it just to look at it." Finally, she told her, "Money is just paper. The most important thing is how you choose to *use* that million dollars." As sweet as that sounds, many adults are just like that little girl, and it's a problem I see in many adults. We get lost in the idea that a set amount of money will bring us happiness and get us everything we want, but we don't put enough time and effort into thinking about what we want to do with our money, which makes us happy.

*It's not all about the money you have, no matter the amount; it's what you do with it that matters. The money would be nothing, "Just paper" without meaning or purpose for it.*

**It's not all about the money you have, no matter the amount; it's what you do with it that matters. The money would be nothing, "Just paper" without meaning or purpose for it.**

MONEY IS NOTHING IF YOU HAVE NO MEANING

Ask yourself, "What is my money truly for?

Is it for romantic getaways with your partner? Is it for taking classes that will help you to develop your mind and body? The ability to volunteer your time and professional expertise to a cause that benefits your community? Seed money to grow your own business?

Your life will take on a brilliant turn when you start to use your means in a meaningful way.

You may become confused about what you want to achieve with money if you don't have clear goals, and you may find yourself stuck. Clear objectives can provide you with tremendous momentum and a strong sense of purpose for your money.

Remember, these aren't work goals that will get you fired if you don't meet them, nor are your boss's goals set for you.

Know what you want to accomplish. You can't plan a route to get somewhere if you don't know where you're going. You'll develop the goals that will help you get there once you have a clear and correct idea of where you want to go and what you want to accomplish. Write down the things that you want to do and would regret not being able to do or have.

**Don't Be Vague. Be specific**

Can you tell where you would be in 5 years? Take the time to sit down and brainstorm your long-term dreams and desires.

**Set your timeline**

Setting deadlines will help you avoid procrastination and motivate you to achieve your objectives. Having a timeline for your goals also aids in their clarification because you now know what you want and when you want it.

**Make a list of goals you want to achieve in a month, a year, and even five or ten years**.

Make a clear plan to keep you on track, but don't etch your plan in stone!! Allow for changes along the way, but don't lose sight of your main goal. Keep in mind a clear goal is a realistic one. This helps you stay on track, and you won't stress yourself out trying to accomplish something that's out of reach

**Use Your Goals to Make Value-Based Decisions**

Make money decisions that are in line with your values and goals. Once you mastered this, money decisions will come quickly to you.

Your objectives serve as a benchmark against which all unnecessary items can be measured. When you come across something you want but don't need, consider whether it is more important to you to achieve your goals or not. Is it possible that I'm feeding an emotion?

Remember, when you choose to honor your goals and values, you cannot deprive yourself of anything. Allow yourself to be frustrated or disappointed if you don't get everything you want; instead, focus on what you do get—the things that are most important to you. And those are things that are indeed worth making conscious money decisions for.

**Live a Rich Life**

In the end, money is just paper. All that matters is what you do with that paper. Give your money purpose -This is what determines whether you'd get more money or go broke. Whether you have one million dollars or significantly less, make decisions that honor your values and goals and leave the legacy you desire.

# CHAPTER 6

# BRILLIANT SUCCESS

It's not who you are to have brilliant success but what you don't do that holds you back

Which came first, the chicken or the egg? To be or not to be? Nature versus Nurture?

Can we finally put this long-running debate to rest and conclude?

IS SUCCESS A FUNCTION OF WHO YOU ARE OR WHAT YOU DO?

True, some people are distinguished by their tenacity, productivity, and dedication. They are lauded for their outstanding achievements and are held up as shining examples of extraordinary success.

The issue is that there are only a few examples to choose from. Meanwhile, the vast majority of people do not have personal success stories.

Is this to imply there is a closed elite club to which only a select few have access?

Definitely not.

If you are an entrepreneur, Trust me, you can be like one of those people who is your inspiration. Successful people are born like one of us; they are not born with some extraordinary power. If they can make things happen, so can we. There's nothing to be afraid of. Remember these few things, and believe me, you can be one amongst successful people.

Remember that there is always a clear-cut difference between the successful and the unsuccessful. John Paul DeJoria, the billionaire behind Paul Michell hair products and Patron tequila, explains what a 'successful' person is: The difference in habits and decisions gives birth to what is being discussed or what is not. "Successful people do all the things that unsuccessful people don't want to do. It has absolutely nothing to do with who they are.

Hard work, perseverance, and determination are all factors that contribute to success. It extends beyond a desire to succeed to taking action to make a difference.

People, for some reason, do not commit to their dreams and postpone the realization of their ideas when it comes to taking a bold step in business. They lament a lack of productivity, inspiration, and good fortune. They eventually settle for a mediocre life, second-rate achievements, and a large number of unfulfilled ambitions.

They do this not because of fierce competition, a lack of time, or knowledge. In most cases, the true enemies are much more straightforward. They appear whenever you start a new business project. They paralyze you and prevent you from acting. The good news is that you can overcome them if you acknowledge and confront them rather than deny the truth.

You must learn about your enemies — the things that are preventing you from achieving success. It will alter the way you approach daily tasks as well as long-term objectives. The better you understand them, the easier it will be to combat them.

## Procrastination

From the moment your idea is born, you begin deferring the start of its realization until "better times."

You always think about it, but you never do anything about it. You appear to be waiting for a miracle, for a bolt of inspiration and energy to strike you and motivate you to act.

It's not going to work out. There has never been a better time to act. Now is the best time.

Once you've come up with an idea, devote some time to conducting initial research to confirm its validity. The sooner you get started, the faster you'll be able to enjoy the fruits of your labor.

Allowing yourself to put things off until later is a recipe for disaster. Make it a habit to act. There will never be a better time to realize your vision or complete your current task. The best time to act is right now.

When you overthink, you usually end up with a slew of doubts that force you to reconsider your decision. All of those failure statistics, your friends' stories, and even a bad weather forecast can quickly become a source of doubt.

You should be unconcerned about someone else's failure. It happened to someone else, not you. Your friends' advice should not bother you either. They usually have no idea what they're talking about. The dangers should not bother you too much. Opportunities, on the other hand, would inspire you.

Stop second-guessing yourself. You're smarter than you think and more powerful than you think.

## Fear

All of those unfounded doubts can quickly turn into fears. You become afraid of taking the first step as a result of your uncertainty.

Fear is what makes you paralyzed and prevents you from acting.

The only way to get rid of your fears is to take action. You can only enter your

Uncomfortable zone and expand your comfort zone by taking confident action.

Fear is the thing that keeps you from achieving your goals. You automatically postpone the realization of your dreams every time you put off meeting your fears. You've taken the first step toward conquering your fears, and you're already halfway there.

## Distraction

Distraction is unquestionably one of the most dangerous enemies of young entrepreneurs and beginners in various fields. While working on the project, it is critical to remain focused and committed. Every achievement is the result of focus and dedication.

Your concentration is lost every time you shift your focus to another object. You lose track of ideas and thoughts that have been running through your mind for the past few minutes. Then it takes some time to regain your focus and get back to work. It simply reduces your productivity and degrades your performance.

The only way to stay productive and consistently produce high-quality results is to stay focused on the current workflow with all of your attention.

Make a schedule for yourself to work on your project. Decide where you want to work. It must be a time and place where you feel at ease working and where you know no one will bother you. Turn off your phone and don't allow yourself to be interrupted by unwanted calls or messages.

**Get to work and finish what you've started.**

It can be challenging to set and achieve meaningful goals. Many people drop out of goals in the middle because they can't keep up the momentum. When you try to achieve ambitious long-term goals, all of your growth enemies are amplified. Short-term planning and interim goals prove to be a great solution in this situation.

Small victories and achieving milestones will help you maintain momentum and remain committed throughout the journey.

To make the most of your objectives, you must concentrate on the result. And to do so, you must be sure of the actions you are taking. You can gain more momentum by breaking down your big goal into smaller, more manageable tasks. You will also gain the necessary motivation to continue pushing forward without giving up. You have a strong desire to improve and grow.

The good news is that you can fight back against your foes.

Now that you've gotten to know them a little better, it's time to show you're brave enough to face them and slay them mercilessly. Fight for increased output. Strive for more outstanding achievements. Fight for what you want!

# CHAPTER 7

# ALWAYS KNOW THAT RELATIONSHIPS ARE MORE IMPORTANT THAN MONEY

Yep, it was Sunday morning, and it was just me, my 80s/90s cheesy music, and my thoughts.

I noticed a recurring theme during my drive. I became aware of how much I had thought about my various relationships over the years, and I realized something I had suspected on some level: relationships are far more important than money.

**Let's talk about it; I'm assuming you agree.**

Relationships are one of the most potent motivators a person can have. When you want to be happy, you need to be able to experience love. However, some people are less concerned about relationships and love than others. Some people seem to be more concerned with making money than with their love lives, and they appear to prioritize financial success over their love lives.

You see, you shouldn't have to go through life without a good relationship. The majority of people have loved ones whom they adore. Even if you don't have a romantic partner, you are most likely loved by friends or family. Having people who care about you allows you to enjoy the true pleasures of life.

Having a strong family bond can make a significant difference in your overall happiness. It's even better when you have someone who can share your joy with you. It's also beneficial to have someone you can rely on during difficult times, making it easier to get through difficult times.

According to a study conducted, "good friends protect people from mental and physical decline, and give a better clue of how long someone's life will be than their social class, IQ or genes." Tell me that statement isn't powerful. Whoa.

I'm becoming more aware of how quickly time passes as I grow older. I'm starting to notice how quickly days turn into years, and years turn into decades.

When you have strong bonds with so many people, you would feel safe in your world. Let's face it. I'm not going to turn to my social media platform for comfort when a crisis occurs. Instead, I'm going to call a trusted family member or friend to talk things over. I've used this strategy to achieve great success many times throughout my life.

This means that the people with whom we have strong bonds have a fantastic way of making us feel as if everything will be okay even when we are in a less-than-ideal situation.

## MONEY IS NOTHING MORE THAN A TOOL.

Of course, I am not implying that money is nothing. I believe that money is crucial and that it should be prioritized in planning and decision-making. On the other hand, money becomes a tool to live a less stressful and more satisfying life once your financial systems are in place to meet your goals.

As important as money is, it can't be compared to loving relationships. Money is only be used for three things: spending, saving, and giving. This statement is correct.

***See how it works***

### SPEND IT

When we spend money on things and people we care about, it can give us a lot of pleasure. I find that spending money on other people gives me a lot more fun than spending money on myself. I've also noticed that spending money on experiences provides me with long-lasting memories, such as our Disney vacation or a cook out with close relatives and friends.

It's a significant change from how I operated, but it's a good one, in my opinion.

Experiment with your thoughts: Consider spending money on an unforgettable vacation with someone you care about to a destination of your choice. Those memories would be priceless and would last a lifetime.

**SAVE IT**

Saving money can be tedious, which is probably why so many people struggle with it. Saving money, on the other hand, leads to financial stability. You'll have one less thing to worry about when you're financially secure.

Consider this scenario: You're sitting there reading this with $1 million or more in your bank account. I'm not a psychic, but I'm willing to bet you'd feel a lot more secure and perhaps even enjoy having more options in life.

**GIVE IT**

One of the best uses of money is to give it away. Giving cash allows you to provide an opportunity to someone who otherwise would not have one.

Consider this hypothetical scenario: You've saved enough money to send your son, daughter, niece, or nephew to their Dream College or technical school. I will go out on a limb and say you won't be disappointed. As and employer and Entrepreneur, I speak from personal experience giving is the most humbling and amazing feeling.

Being in a position to create a opportunity to give someone a chance to better there situation, or change their life is not only Beneficial to them but also To you and your growth.

Did you notice how money is disposable in the three essential uses of money?

## OKAY, WITH THAT SAID, WHAT MATTERS IN THE END?

In the end, what matters is that you live a fulfilling life with the people you value the most. Those experiences and memories will mean just as much, if not more, to the next generation than the money you leave behind.

### CONCLUSION

Remember, when you die, you can't take it with you. When you have a terrible day, a wad of cash will never comfort you. I don't care if you're the richest man in the universe, but money can't make you happy, and you can't go out to dinner or vacation with your bank account.

# CHAPTER 8

# FINANCIAL LITERACY

Knowledge equals wisdom and wisdom equals power .

Did you know there's a huge difference between being poor and being broke?

Broke is just temporary because it is solely a financial set back.

Sadly poor is ever lasting because it's a combination of ones mindset , lifestyle, and habits .

What do you understand about Financial Literacy, and Why Is It Important?

Consider financial literacy to be the process of making friends with your money. The sooner you get to know each other, the faster you'll be able to achieve your objectives.

What you do with your money today — how you spend, save, and develop money habits — can have a long-term impact on your financial well-being and relationships.

Money management is a crucial life skill that can assist you in achieving your objectives and living more comfortably. When you understand how to make the most of your money, a whole new world of possibilities opens up for you. Don't waste any more time! The sooner you begin to develop your financial literacy, the sooner you will reap the benefits of your growing financial knowledge.

In case you were wondering, financial literacy is the ability to manage money effectively. Simply put, financial literacy refers to knowledge of financial concepts such as budgeting, saving, investing, and debt and credit management. A financially literate person knows how to make and stick to a budget, what features to look for when they open a new saving or checking account, how to pay off debt, and set an appropriate emergency fund goal. How to invest in stocks, bonds, and mutual funds is an example of advanced financial literacy.

It's important to remember that financial literacy doesn't happen overnight; once you've mastered the fundamentals, you can continue to expand your knowledge as your circumstances change. For example, financial literacy can help you make informed daily financial decisions (Can I afford to go out to lunch today?). Is it okay if I put this pair of jeans on my credit card?) As well as long-term goals (How much should I set aside each month for retirement?).

You can assess your financial literacy by asking yourself the following questions:

- Do I know how to make a monthly budget and stick to it?
- Is it possible for me to make a plan for saving for multiple goals at the same time?
- Do I know how different financial decisions affect my credit score?
- Would I know how to compare financing options if I were buying a car?

After considering your priorities, you can start looking for resources to help you improve your financial literacy in those areas.

## What are the benefits of expanding your financial knowledge?

Learning how to manage your money now will lay a solid foundation for your financial success in the future. The more INSIGHT you have about personal finance, the more confident you'll be when it comes to building a solid emergency fund, paying off debt, buying a car or home, investing (short- and long-term), and planning for retirement. Financial literacy can make your life easier by assuring you that you are making wise, well-informed financial decisions.

A lack of financial knowledge, on the other hand, can make life more difficult. You may, for example, put yourself at greater risk of debt, bankruptcy, foreclosure, or fraud. Any of these pitfalls can get in the way of achieving your objectives.

Like any other form of education, financial literacy is intended to assist you in bettering yourself, making better decisions, and achieving success in whatever path you choose.

**Financial education has five components.**

1. **Budgeting Fundamentals**

One of the most fundamental aspects of staying on top of your finances is creating and maintaining a budget. With the aid of websites and apps like Mint.com, it's easier than ever to create a budget in today's world. It doesn't matter if math isn't your strong suit; these user-friendly tools can help anyone stay on track with their finances. They'll also keep you informed about where your money is going if you use them correctly.

You may find it challenging to keep track of where your money comes from and what you spend on if you don't stick to a budget. Any financial novice should start by learning the fundamentals of budgeting.

2. **Savings as a Priority**

Savings is, without a doubt, an important part of keeping a healthy financial situation. However, most businesses and households do not place as much emphasis on this as they should. It's easy to overlook things like retirement because it seems so far away. Early savings education can help you gain the knowledge, practice, and set of skills you'll need for the rest of your life.

If this is a new concept for you, start with the simplest example: saving money for a higher-ticket item. Working toward a goal is critical, and you must recognize the importance of paying yourself first – because bills will always be there. Do you feel at ease? That comes with time, effort, and patience, all of which you'll develop as you master your savings skills.

Set a small savings goal for yourself, your family, and your business to begin with. It could be $5 or $10 per week. Once you've reached your initial goal, whatever you decide, increase the amount you save each week. Having a "rainy day fund" in your account is also a good idea. This is the money you can use if your car's air conditioning breaks down or you need to purchase unexpected home equipment.

3. **Identity Theft Concerns & Security**

Identity theft is more rampant than ever before in today's world. Your financial information is more vulnerable to fraud now that everything is digital, and almost everyone has shopped online at some point.

Understanding this concept and preventative measures such as password protection and limiting the amount of information shared online can be the difference between having safe accounts and having them ruined.

While it's not a foolproof science (people can be safe and bad things still happen), it's critical to protect your finances as much as possible to avoid the risks that exist. Never, ever, ever use your credit card in a public place. To make those purchases, wait until you get home.

Finally, make sure that your passwords are secure. An uppercase letter, lowercase letter, number, and symbol are usually required for a strong password.

# CHAPTER 9

# VALUE YOUR VISION YOUR

## VISION SHOULD BE THE FOCUS.

When building your business, your heart's desire and passion served as the basis. But when was the last time you picked up a pen to record your mission on paper (or type it in on a keyboard)?

If your answer is "yesterday," I take my hat off to you. So please give me a little moment to bow to you with the appropriate ceremony. (This includes, among other things, a dance with complete choreography.)

But if it's been a while longer, we should look at how it is easy to get to the point of what you stand for.

You see, you need to value your vision, else you'd be lost. Even the Bible says people perish because they lack vision. Ask yourself, "What WOULD YOU LIKE to achieve?"

It's about your most ambitious dreams for your business or company. Let's assume you run a yoga studio, and your vision is to help people be happier and more balanced in their lives in general. Or you are an accountant and see your task as finally giving your customers financial freedom. Or juggler who teaches people how to throw clothes in the air and thus revolutionize standard meditation practices.

Whatever you do, you already have a vision. Now is the time to put this vision into words, and this is how you value it. My vision is, _______________, so that _______________.

**When you recognize and value those visions, it commands ACTION. Your vision works hand in hand with your mission so let's talk about it.**

**Your mission**

If you've answered the question "what would you like to achieve," the question arises:

How do I realize this vision? What logistical, concrete steps can you take to achieve these abstract dreams?

Take, for example, the owner of the yoga studio. In the long term, his vision is to help people to be more satisfied and balanced in their lives in general. His mission could be to open an inviting yoga studio where everyone is welcome.

The accountant mentioned above would like to show his customers how to gain financial freedom. The first step is to operate a successful tax consulting company for other entrepreneurs.

**Ask yourself: Does this bring me closer to my mission, and does it help me to realize my vision?**

Identifying your vision and mission makes it much easier for you to make strategic decisions regarding your company. Keep learning and focus on knowing what you want - and how exactly you achieve it.

**Next, Name the values of your company**

Or put another way: Write down all the traits of your business or company that you admire.

Unlike your mission, values are not tangible goals or plans. Instead, it is probably more about the most important characteristics of your company. Are you primarily interested in sustainability? Transparency? Engagement? Respect?

Take a moment and think about the

Values that are close to your heart professionally - and probably also privately. Once you have defined three or four values, they become your leitmotifs that determine everything else: your logo's design to your service.

## Take time to emphasize the charms of your company so that you can enchant your customers later.

Working on your mission and vision is an excellent opportunity to rediscover what you do best, breathe new energy into your company, and remember that you are the person who determines the processes in your company. You make the rules - this applies in particular to the strategy and branding of your small business.

On this basis, you can fine-tune the basics of your brand. You can focus better, be more motivated, and recognize how you present yourself in this strange and wonderful world.

### Promote positive thinking and acting!

Peter Drucker said, "Culture eats strategy/tactic for breakfast." That's right. No matter how intelligent and sophisticated a strategy has no chance of implementation, the ruling culture opposes it. Culture cannot be commanded. Culture can only be developed very slowly. But you can make agreements, i.e., draw up guidelines and agree on their compliance.

Behavioral design is the lever to change the culture of a team. Promote, support, and reward positive thinking and agreed action in all areas and with all means at your disposal. This is not so much about financial incentives but appreciation, recognition, and prominent praise. Communicate success stories in-home media. Appreciate positive behavioral changes. Pay your attention to those who actively develop in the spirit of the vision. And: Live out the values, norms, and attitudes of your desired corporate culture!

**Stay stubborn!**

Even if you have an attractive vision for your company's future, the way there is not an easy task. Without perseverance, this will not succeed. Finally, your vision describes how much money your company wants to earn within five, ten, or even fifteen years. It is a marathon for which you need a long breath. It is not uncommon for the achievement of a vision to fail because only rapid success is worked towards, but then energy and endurance are lacking for the entire route.

When you give up on the goal, you have wasted time, strength, money, and resources. You also lose credibility: When you call for the next marathon, fewer employees will be motivated to start. If you have decided on a longer-term goal, you prove persistence. It's worth it! Therefore: Be patient - and remain stubborn!

# CHAPTER 10

# POWER IS NOTHING WITHOUT PURPOSE.

Every motivational speaker emphasizes the significance of having a life purpose. They all tell you that living a life without a purpose regardless of what position you occupy is a bad idea.

There isn't a single one of them who is incorrect. Everything they say is correct.

There is absolutely no point in having power if you don't know what you're doing. Have you read Neil Gaiman's Norse Mythology, a retelling of some of Odin's, Thor's, Loki's, and other Norse gods' stories? You'd notice a lack of purpose in their lives time and time again. They had incredible power, but they lacked any overarching sense of purpose, so they used it in strange ways that were usually harmful to others.

Let's make this more personal. If you look at most of today's superhero movies, you'll notice that, while they're entertaining, they typically lack the depth of character worth exploring. At best, these characters are on a mission to save the world because, well, "great power comes with great responsibility." Still, it appears to be more of an emotionally charged job description than a genuine desire for human flourishing.

Some people have power, which they should use for the betterment of the world and human flourishing.

Power without a purpose, like a life without a goal, is destructive and wasteful.

## A life without meaning is meaningless.

Have you ever feared leading a life that was devoid of meaning? If not, you have no idea how excruciating such a life can be.

Imagine not wanting to get up in the morning but also not wanting to go to bed. There was no desire to work, no desire to spend, no desire to enjoy the company of friends, and no reason to live. A mind that is blank and has nothing to think about. The absence of negative and positive emotions. There isn't anything to look forward to.

Yes, life is depressing. That's how you'll feel if you don't have a goal in life.

A lack of goals indicates a lack of purpose. This means that nothing is pointing you in the direction of a fictitious final destination. You have nowhere to go, it's excruciating to be on the road, and you don't even care for the route.

Consider it from the standpoint that you do have a defined purpose in life for a clearer picture. You put your trust in life in every way. What exactly does that imply? It motivates you to work harder. You get closer to your final destination with each step you take. This automatically encourages you to improve your performance.

You'll never be able to scale your achievements if you don't have a goal. You dismiss it as meaningless because you have no idea where it is leading you. However, when you're well aware of the expected outcomes, even the least progress can be motivating.

You can try all of the motivation-boosting techniques, but the most effective is discovering and living your life's purpose.

## You can't grow if you're not focused.

Growth is required in every field, career, aspect of life, and relationship. Human life is about progress—if nothing else, your mental capacity and knowledge expand.

What is the source of this expansion? You could have access to the most up-to-date information. You won't learn a word unless your mind is in the right frame of mind to absorb it. Similarly, even the most insignificant events can teach you something useful if you are focused.

Essentially, having a life purpose keeps you working in the same direction. You can tweak things here and there, but the result is predictable. So, in the grand scheme of things, all of your hard work aims to fulfill your life's purpose.

It is impossible to achieve this level of concentration in any other way. You'll choose a career path, people in your life, relationships, friends, living space, and even your daily commute with a purpose in mind. As a result, your focus is unaffected wherever you go. Consistently keep the end goal in mind.

You can quickly get past minor inconveniences if you keep your focus on the right things. The important things, no matter how little, are always in your mind. Overall, a person with a defined life purpose finds it much easier to work well, harder, and more effectively.

What's more amazing is that people who lack a sense of purpose in life are 2.4 times more likely to develop Alzheimer's disease.

The reason for this could be that people who lack a sense of purpose in life lose hope and have nothing to look forward to. As a result, the psychological effect has an impact on their physical health. In any case, why wouldn't you want to have a defined life purpose if it can save you from all of this stress?

## Nothing is enjoyable in life.

A large part of one's life purpose is to be socially included. People who have no purpose in life are more likely to be lonely. Even if they attend social events, they are less likely to enjoy themselves.

Because such people lack mental clarity, they are unable to enjoy the enjoyable activities that surround them. Emotions are incomprehensible to their brain. This isn't to say that their circumstances aren't satisfactory. For someone who is mentally satisfied, the same environment and people can be enjoyable.

## Conclusion

Every single one of these reasons has been proven to be the result of a life without direction. Every reason contributes to a chaotic lifestyle. Nobody would choose to live a life like that on purpose.

We only have a limited amount of time to live in this world. So, rather than squandering it by living a life without meaning, it's time to make an effort to improve it.

It is within your power to free yourself from this torturous existence. Put up with the hassle and short-term struggle to live a worthy life for the rest of your life!

## CHAPTER 11

# PROPER PREPARATION PREVENT POOOR PERFORMANCE

The phrase "proper preparation prevents poor performance" is one we should repeat to ourselves frequently to remind ourselves of the importance of planning. We cannot hope to perform at a high level if we do not prepare for our week, whether it is a sporting event or the workweek.

The Five P's are as follows: Former Secretary of State James Baker said, "Prior preparation prevents poor performance."

It's all a matter of perspective. There is a level of performance that is superior to the majority. There's also an intentional performance at a high level to motivate you to be the best you can be. The "Five P's" can help you remember that more planning equals better results.

Many of us don't plan or prepare ourselves for anything serious. We wake up in the morning and allow the day to run us along its course, not running it the way we have planned. We leave everything to chance, and we are often left in the lurch.

Unfortunately, some of us have more self-control than others. The majority of us aren't professional "preparers." It takes a distinct kind of determination to thoroughly prepare every time, and those who do so stand out.

We believe we want to accomplish something many times in life but refuse to prepare for it properly. We think it is possible, but it rarely occurs. Preparation has a direct impact on the outcome. Poor planning almost always leads to disappointment. Poor performance can be avoided with proper preparation!

According to Aristotle, "We are what we repeatedly do," excellence is a habit, not an act." Excellence is never a result of chance.

*Allow me to tell you a story....*

This is a story about a farmer who was interviewing a potential employee. He inquired as to the young man's most valuable asset. "I can sleep when the wind starts blowing," the young man explained. The farmer had no idea what he meant, but he hired the young man anyway.

A few weeks later, during the night, strong wind and rainstorm blew in. The farmer quickly grabbed his flashlight and went out to the large barn to check everything was working in order. The windmill had been turned off and the lever down. The cows had been bedded down in the neat straw. The straw pile had been secured with a canvas firmly tied down over the top, and the barn doors and shutters had been tightly closed and barred.

The farmer then went into the bunkhouse and discovered the young man soundly sleeping. He finally understood what the young man meant when he said, "I can sleep when the wind blows."

Marcus Mariota, for example. I'm sure you've heard about how he won 23 games in two years as the quarterback at Oregon? He's a strong contender for the Heisman Trophy this year. He's been named "the country's best-prepared football player." He already knew the entire Oregon playbook when he arrived as a freshman! His performance is a reflection of his Preparation.

Behind every successful goal is a solid plan and Preparation towards it. Also, behind most failures are inadequate preparations.

You see, "He who fails to prepare, prepares to fail, and every properly planned program will give the attendees the best show. In high school and college, there were some classes where the teacher would surprise everyone with a "pop quiz." It was impossible to predict when the test would be given. You'd be anxious and afraid if you weren't prepared, but if you were, you'd get a good grade and enjoy the class. Be a dream chaser, and do not relent in chasing your dream.

Many people have failed in life because they lack proper Preparation for many great things that could have benefited them. Procrastination and lack of focus has led to many downfalls, so make hay while the sun shines.

Proper Preparation is required in making some vital life decisions such as choosing a partner, saving for college or graduation, starting a new business, taking risks, etc.

Take, for instance, savings; frugality is one of the things I learned during my preparation stage in entrepreneurship. Let me explain further

**Frugality is a sign of preparedness, not saving money.**

Being financially prepared for the future means spending within your means and putting a significant portion of your income aside.

Many veterans' futures are uncertain, and one of the first realities they face once they return to civilian life is that they have responsibilities and bills to pay. Any veteran who learns how to live frugally will have something set aside in the event of a rainy day.

**Education**

One of the things you can do to prepare yourself is to get an education. While this may not appear to be an obvious way to prepare, I disagree.

One of the most effective ways to prepare for any eventuality is to educate yourself. If you have a university degree to back you up, you will have a much better chance of landing a high-paying job once you leave the nest and enter the work force.

When you eventually enter that world, attending seminars, conferences, or even listening to podcasts on fields and areas that interest you will provide you with some level of knowledge and know-how.

**Developing Self-Control**

What role does this play in Preparation -getting up early, scheduling time for exercise, and working hard to achieve goals? If you ask me, this plays a massive role in preparing.

Discipline is one of the most effective forms of self-preparation that each of us can provide.

When you put yourself in a state where you are creating good habits and conditioning your body to be in the best possible shape, you prepare yourself for any eventuality and create an environment that is more conducive to success. Additionally, sticking to a routine cuts down on wasted time and allows you to accomplish more in a given day.

"Be prepared," says a good boy scout. "Be ready," says the Bible. "Proper preparation prevents poor performance," says a good coach.

The preparation period is now!

# CHAPTER 12

# CONFIDENCE WITHOUT CLARITY IS DANGEROUS

Did you know that many authors write the endings of books first before they begin? They begin with the end in mind - CLARITY OF PURPOSE OR INTENT.

Many people never start considering who/where they want to be as long as they have confidence. As a result, they are never able to realize their personal or professional goals. Unfortunately, some businesses today are in a similar situation.

Unknown to them, confidence without Clarity is a disaster, an absolute disaster in life. It is just that sometimes confidence works —that's the whole problem. This kind of confidence is usually a result of a strong belief system, wealth, trust, or pure foolishness. People who have this kind of confidence have no sense of life or hardship. They often leave everything to chance and constantly walk in ignorance. This can be very dangerous.

Imagine there's a busy highway. Without looking to your left and right, you cross the road in confidence that you're going to be safe. You may make it, but there is a high possibility that you will not make it alive or sustain injuries. Even quantum mechanics also says there is a one-in-a-billion chance you may walk through the wall, so you can always make it by chance but isn't that a complete waste of time and an act of foolishness.

So, rather than confidence, a human being requires Clarity. With a clear vision, you know where you're going and how to get there because you're guided by your mind's map and your heart's compass. You can quickly become distracted and lose sight of the opportunities in front of you if you don't have a clear vision. Dealing with the unknown and unexpected, as well as the ups and downs you'll encounter along the path to achieving your vision, becomes difficult.

If you know where you are now and where you want to go in life, you must have a clear vision because those with a clear vision are more likely to succeed. You can't grow today or in the future, if you don't have a clear vision. You'll realize that having a clear vision in life is just as important as eating good food and breathing clean air.

Recognize that a lack of Clarity, not necessarily your confidence, but your abilities and willingness to see beyond may limit your ability to achieve your objectives. As a result, having a clear vision is critical.

According to a wise man, if you could make all of your major life decisions by tossing a coin, you'd flip its head one way, and its tail the other. It may only work half of the time!

If you are correct, 50% of the time, you can only pursue two professions: weatherman or astrologer. You would almost certainly be fired in any other job. This shows you that confidence without Clarity will lead to disaster.

You need Clarity of purpose and vision to see where you're going. When you begin to see your destination from the beginning, you will be successful and happy in life. This will enable you to keep your eyes on the ball and prevent you from making costly mistakes in business and life generally.

## THE IMPORTANCE OF CLARITY

Clarity can be equated to having a good vision. And this is a mental image of the results you want to achieve—-one that is so clear and vivid that it will aid in making that outcome a reality. Clarity is not a wish, a dream, or a hope in the abstract. It's a depiction of real-world outcomes from real-world efforts. It arrives from the future, energizes, and informs the present. Clarity of purpose is the most powerful tool of all time, and a man with this toll is a confident man. Confidence relies on Clarity.

**Here's why Clarity is so powerful:**

Clarity motivates people to take action. A compelling vision attracts people, ideas, and other resources. It generates the motivation and energy to effect change. It motivates people and organizations to commit, persevere, and give their all.

Clarity helps keep organizations and groups focused and together, especially with complex projects and in stressful times.

CLARITY comes from the heart, not confidence. Don't try to think your way to Clarity. Clarity renders the phrase "fake it till you make it useless. Realize that with Clarity, you begin with the end in mind.

## Begin with the End in Mind

Begin each day, assignment, or project with a clear understanding of your desired direction and destination. If you do this for 30 days, you'd have a great chance of achieving your goals and objectives. Once you've decided where you want to go (Clarity), you can consider the steps you'll need to take or the objectives you'll need to meet to arrive at your desired location. Clarity of vision brings your objectives into focus and moves your ideas into the real world.

So, in short, to begin with, CLARITY entails planning your life and career in the direction you want it to go before you start pursuing it. You will have more control over your life and circumstances if you choose to do so. As a result, you will not be like a fool who embarks on a journey without knowing where they are going. You'll also benefit from improved vision clarity, which will reveal what you want.

This improved Clarity of vision will allow you to be more efficient and effective in your actions, allowing you to understand your purpose better.

It's time for a change. You owe it to yourself. Make this season the season that propels you to get closer to fulfilling your vision for your life.

# CHAPTER 13

# SELF LOVE

## Making myself happy!

Self-love - isn't that something for esoteric and egoists? Not at all! Taking care of yourself as you are is one of the most critical prerequisites for happiness. But how does it succeed in loving oneself? A few insights help with this.

Have you ever wondered why you can hardly deal with stress? Why does everyday life consume so much strength? Why does life make life so much easier for others? Why do others manage to deal with stress and problems better? Why do others seem to be able to enjoy the beautiful things in life much more than you? Maybe you think that the others are simply stronger, more resilient, more beautiful, brighter, and happier than you? Stop! No one should talk about you like that - not even yourself. Maybe the truth is simple: Everyday life consumes too much of your strength because it is simply too much. Or because you demand too much due to too high demands.

**How do I talk to myself?**

If you talk to yourself very hard and badly more often, your inner critic is particularly pronounced. This negative inner voice is a common indication of low self-esteem and too little self-love. Sometimes even a glance in the mirror reveals what self-love is like: If you pay attention to your supposed flaws, you become increasingly dissatisfied with yourself. This also applies to inner workings: Instead of helping you in challenging times and removing the pressure, the inner voice becomes a strict supervisor that makes life even harder for you. Because blame, anxiety, and complaints will always make you feel worse. They prevent you from gaining distance from a situation to take a new perspective. On the other hand, those who treat themselves with forgiveness and focus on strengths strengthen themselves.

**Why can't I just be happy?**

Most of us feel the desire to be happy and, at the same time, have no idea what makes us happy. Many live their lives as expected of them, have specific requirements and are looking for happiness outside: a smart car, a good job, a great partner, an exciting hobby, an exciting trip, recognition of others. Too often, we succumb to the fallacy that we have to achieve specific goals first to be happy. But we have to realize that material possessions and a life in which you have "everything" do not make us an optimistic person by a long shot.

Serious diseases such as addiction and depression have many causes, but usually, one thing in common: lack of self-love because **the key to happiness is to love yourself.** To accept oneself with all facets, with weaknesses and strengths. This does not mean approving and justifying mistakes and shortcomings, but accepting them. Forgive your mistakes and learn from them instead of constantly pretending to be. To console oneself instead of reproaching. Opportunities for yourself to recognize where crises arise.

Recognizing oneself for his nature and his deeds and to say to oneself: You are good enough. You give the best that is currently possible for you.

Our parents lay the foundation for healthy self-esteem in early childhood. If love and attention are subject to certain conditions, we learn over time: We have to do something to be loved.

**Where does lack of self-love come from?**

Our parents lay the foundation for healthy self-esteem in early childhood. If they accept, strengthen, and love us unconditionally, good self-esteem can develop. Self-love arises when we are unconditionally loved by our parents and the people around us. This is by no means always the case. Because to prepare children for life, parents often mistakenly attach their love to conditions. We must be good, obedient, ambitious, and friendly. Otherwise, the parents will not love us.

We want to meet the conditions well because then the dad, the mom, the internalized parents promise us affection. By internalized parents, it means the relationship traces that our parents leave us for a lifetime and project on others. If love and attention are linked to certain conditions, such as good performance and adapted behavior, we learn over time: We have to do something to be loved.

Conversely, unfortunately, this often implies that we are not adorable if we do something, do not achieve it, or lose something again. And that we still have to make a little more effort to be recognized and loved. Therefore, a pronounced "inner critic" does not necessarily speak the truth, but he says what you have learned and internalized in the course of life. Beliefs such as "I can't do this," "I'm not good enough," "I'm not smart enough," "I have to persevere" form the breeding ground for self-doubt and prevent self-love from developing. They also lead us to seek attention, confirmation, and love from outside because we have not learned how to give ourselves all this.

## There is hope: self-love can be learned.

It is a process that sometimes lasts for years, but once you have started it, you will quickly feel positive effects.

**What do I have to change?**

You don't have to do anything! Self-love is not self-optimization but self-acceptance. Those who learn to love themselves stand up for themselves and do not give up. Sometimes this means saying yes to yourself and no to others. Don't make self-love another project in a stressful phase of life - rather listen to yourself instead of thinking everything up, implement mini-steps instead of planning a profound change. Self-love is a process that takes time.

Learn to ask the right questions. Inspire yourself by questioning your thoughts and your heart. The answers themselves are irrelevant.

When was the last time I laughed tears? Who impressed me deeply and why? What life do I want to tell my grandchildren about? Who am I? Where do I want to go? What do I need for my everyday life to be satisfied? And what is the difference to happiness? Which values are important to me? Why am I thinking about what others think? In whose life can I make a difference? If the thoughts are free, why do I limit them with my own beliefs? Do I live my own life or that of the others, whom

I can never wholly please anyway? Who would I like to tell me what he means to me and why don't I do it today? What am I grateful for?

**How can I learn to love myself?**

**Perceive**

Feel how you are doing within you - without evaluating. Every feeling can be there.

**Feel**

Allow yourself your feelings. They are simply there and want to be felt. Only then can they dissolve and transform.

**Watch**

Which event triggers which feeling in you? What needs do I have right now? Write down your observations.

**Reflect**

When are you satisfied or dissatisfied with yourself? What role do your thoughts play? When do you talk badly to yourself?

**Be vigilant**

Watch what's happening inside you. Open yourself and your heart to new experiences, to change, and to unknown feelings.

**Practice**

Wanting to love yourself and doing it is not the same. Nobody says it's easy - but it's worth every try, every effort, and every moment for you. You are worth it.

**Learn**

Read, listen or see how other people practice self-love and what tips they have for you. The more your mind deals with it. The more your heart opens up to new perspectives.

**Love**

Do something good for yourself more often. Take time for yourself and your relationship with yourself. Be forgiving and loving with yourself.

**Practical tips for more self-love: Choose what suits you!**

- Realign your short-term and long-term goals
- Take time for yourself, make dates with yourself and learn to see loneliness as something positive that can strengthen you.
- Feel physical - through sport, sensuality, and relaxation techniques
- Change your beliefs
- Self-love does not mean self-optimization: Do something good often, be patient with yourself, and take care of yourself.

- Exchange ideas with like-minded people
- Write down wise sayings, little wisdom, new insights, your thinking blocks.
- Think about what your values are and then act
- Find contact with your inner child, for example, through meditation
- Say no to others and affirm your worth: You don't have to sacrifice yourself constantly and offer your help
- Do more of what you love
- Get in touch with your heart: Sometimes music can help to allow feelings
- Live the way you think it's right - and not the way others want it
- Question your actions: Which actions are good for you?
- Be good to yourself and be forbearance!
- Write down what you like about yourself
- Smile at your reflection
- Understand what you want - and learn to communicate and stand up for it
- Show others your limits instead of letting them cross

# CHAPTER 14

# RUN YOUR RELATIONSHIP AS YOU WOULD A BUSINESS

Do you treat your relationship as if it were a business?

And I don't mean it in a cold, indifferent, or impassionate way when I ask the question. Are you as invested in your relationship as you are in your job or business?

Everyone, after all, deserves to be with someone they can love and support. You, in turn, are entitled to love and support.

It's exhilarating to fall in love for the first time. It gives you butterflies in your stomach and makes you see the world through rose-colored glasses. If you're in your mid-twenties or early thirties, however, you've probably worked hard to attain your career goals and assure financial security, and you can't afford to let a few butterflies get in the way.

I'll show you how to have a long-lasting and healthy relationship in this section. Building a lifelong relationship isn't difficult, but it isn't simple either. It demands both partners' dedication, commitment, and equal levels of effort.

So, how can we improve our relationship? Manage it as if it were a business.

**A RELATIONSHIP IS AN INVESTMENT.**

Would you put your money into a company venture that was bound to fail? While you may not be investing money in your relationship right away, you are investing time and energy, both of which are incredibly precious resources.

**ABOUT YOUR GOALS, YOU NEED TO BE ON THE SAME PAGE.**

Your relationship will not work if you want to save money for retirement, but your partner wants to "live in the moment." Instead of stagnating, you must find a way to unify your goals and work toward them as a team. You must be on the same page, just like business partners.

**IT TAKES TIME TO GROW.**

Most start-up founders would agree to the reality that any new firm requires care and attention to thrive. It's critical to recognize that the same is true in relationships. The more time and effort you put into your business, the more money you'll make. Patience and getting to know one another are the foundations of solid relationships, which are impossible to attain without time.

**EMOTIONS MUST BE KEPT OUT OF FINANCIAL DECISIONS.**

When you've had a massive blow-out, it's tempting to want to stop paying the cable bill just to spite your lover, but what happens when you kiss and makeup? When it comes to financial decisions, emotions can obscure our judgment. You'll make much better financial decisions if you think about them like a business analyst, considering all conceivable hazards (such as a breakup).

**A PARTNER, NOT JUST A LOVER, IS WHAT YOU REQUIRE.**

When things get rough, you'll need someone who can step in and lend a hand wherever it's needed. To help you develop, you should consider finding a companion that complements your strengths. You're not very good at budgeting? Look for a companion who is. You're not very good with people? Find a spouse who can act as a "social buffer" between you and the rest of the world.

**YOU BOTH HAVE PARTS TO PLAY, AND YOU MUST KNOW WHAT THEY ARE.**

When employees understand what is expected of them, company hierarchies work. To avoid those dreadful, ridiculous conflicts about whose turn it is to do dishes, both of you need to be conscious of your tasks and responsibilities in the relationship — or around the house — and treat them as your work. You'll have more time for each other if you tackle tasks jointly. Knowing what your partner expects of you makes it easier to meet those demands.

**Consultants have a role to play.**

A company might hire an expert or consultant to assist them in a particular area with problems. It should be the same in your relationship. Couples fight, it's inevitable, but if you're ready to seek outside advice, you'll have a much greater chance of making amends and moving on. Couples must accept that they may not always have the skills or resources to complete the job, whether it's from a financial planner or a relationship counselor, and that's fine. However, abandoning up would mean squandering a potentially profitable investment.

# CHAPTER 15

# APPRECIATE YOUR RELATIONSHIP

Have you ever heard the phrase "Appreciate what you have before you end up appreciating what you had?"

Do we appreciate each other in our relationships, or do we take each other for granted, particularly when the honeymoon time has passed, and we've been together for a long, or with our family and friends? We often don't realize we've fallen into a state of lack of care and respect for one another until something happens to shake us up - disagreements, irritation, resentment, affairs – and then we focus on what's wrong with the relationship.

Perhaps a sense of little boredom or that life is just a touch' humdrum,' a little repetitious, with no significant problems or issues, but the luster has worn off a relationship.

So, when was the last time you took a moment to demonstrate your love and appreciation for your partner or loved ones? How can you adequately describe how beautiful and great a relationship is, as well as everything you like about it when it comes to relationships?

It is essential to show this affection repeatedly, with gestures, a friendly smile, nice words, and much more. What you give the other without asking for anything in return often comes back to you.

**How can you express your affection?**

Let your partner know again and again what you like about them! Appreciate him/her for their commitment to work and family, to be together with friends, relatives, acquaintances, etc.

Respect and value their hobbies and preferences - give them enough space for this. Maybe he/she is particularly committed to a non-profit association, supports ecological projects, animal welfare, or other things. So give them enough room for his leisure activities and have confidence in him/her Your partner will love you all the more for that.

**Love frees up - do not control the partner.**

You should avoid control and jealousy. True love, let's go and do not captivate. True love frees up. But first of all, this means that you can also love yourself, take care of yourself as you are, and create your freedom. When you are together again, and exchange ideas about it, joy, connection, and appreciation deepen.

Of course, it is all well and good to do things that you both like together in your free time or even accompany the other if he/she wishes. At the same time, you can also get in touch with the people who are important to your partner and get to know and understand them better and better.

**Show appreciation instead of criticizing.**

So give this trust to your lover over and over again. Express that you want to make them happy and let your partner know that he/she also makes you happy with their being, and whole personality, strengths, and weaknesses. Make sure that you often value each other more than criticize one another.

**Correct criticism without accusations**

Of course, criticism is also part of the partnership, but it should be benevolent. Always tell them in the first-person form what bothered or even hurt you. Avoid the accusation "you are ...., you have ... etc." So you take the sting out of the discussion, and the other will not feel attacked.

This is also an excellent way to express your love. You have confidence in your partner that they values your feelings. Often it is small things that hurt the other, and they are not even aware of it. That's why openness and honesty are part of it.

**Get to know the partner again and again and give them love.**

As you change over time, so does the quality of your love over the years. You may no longer be quite as stormy and enthusiastic as in the early days. And yet, over the years, you gain something precious, something that is only true for both of you, a unique relationship in which you have gone through ups and downs together.

**Gratitude strengthens the relationship.**

Gratitude ENHANCES RELATIONSHIPS. Express them to your partner again and again. Make every day an unforgettable day as if you had just met again. So don't be afraid to give them small gifts now and then, cook something special, show the partner with a bit of attention, and gesture that you are happy to have them by your side.

It is more important to do this now and then as a surprise than just on certain holidays such as birthdays, Christmas, etc. It is precisely the little gestures that the other is happy about and that come back to you. Maybe there is something that your partner mentioned quite casually, which they would be pleased about. Then surprise them with it. And indeed, there are no limits to your imagination to express your love again and again.

*Remember, appreciation can help bring out the greatness and potential in your relationship and re-ignite the love that is there.*

The bottom line is that it's never too late to show your love for one another.

# CHAPTER 16

# DON'T GIVE UP

This advice is primarily based on personal experience after losing a business opportunity with a contract of over three million dollars. I was devastated as I was down to just myself and my kids being a single dad at the time. There was nobody to turn to, and my friends were nowhere to be found. I guess what they say is true about having your own back like no other. In this context, having your own back is being proud of who you are. It entails having faith in oneself. It involves appreciating yourself, even when you make mistakes.

Life had taught me that I am the only one to take myself out of an unpleasant situation. Yes, ***me.*** I knew better than to give up. I had responsibilities, and I had goals. I was fierce and would do everything in my capacity to achieve it.

With this drive, I took a step of faith, obtained a loan (with interest) from a family relative, and started again. I was able to get back on track, and I've grown my business from two employees and nil revenue to several employees and a nearly seven-figure turnover.

Daily, life seems to confront us with an endless number of challenges and issues. It throws left hooks when we expect right angles; it delivers us apples when we want oranges; it even tosses us unexpectedly nasty surprises, and it bloats us with resourceful emotions that bind us to a life of mediocrity and misery.

Despite this, what we do with what occurs to us defines where we would probably wind up, what we will have, and how our experiences will shape us, not what happens to us.

When the oceans are calm and nothing appears to be in our way, it is pretty easy to work toward our goals and ambitions. We panic and struggle to deal with our situations if we are not mentally prepared when anything begins to stir the waters and rock the boat from side to side. These issues and difficulties appear to be larger than life, well beyond our ability and resources.

These incidents may end up overpowering us and creating a tremendous deal of pain and suffering. As a result, we may wind up resigning and throwing in the towel of defeat, all because our resolve wasn't strong enough to withstand the stress of our path toward achieving our goals.

Where can I find the will to continue fighting if it feels like I'm lying on the ground? Where can I find the courage to keep going when I feel like I can no longer face the challenges ahead of me? Is it possible that I am stronger than I believe? These are just a few of the questions you might ask yourself when you go through a difficult phase. And yes, people have developed incredible power and fantastic survival skills.

**We can withstand more pain than we think**. Somewhere we find the motivation to continue when our strength weakens, and everything around us gets dark.

Sometimes we realize how we paved our way, stone by stone, without being aware of how we got so far, despite the pain. Our resistance knows no limits.

But where do we get the strength to pick ourselves up when everything hurts? It lives in us, but sometimes is hidden and difficult to find, giving us only weak signs of existence. Nevertheless, the power is always there in one way or another. Sometimes we only need help to know how to use it.

Our survival instinct and all of the other resources we have and from which we draw energy are responsible for igniting the power within us. But to make this happen, we must listen to our emotions to find out what we need and then act accordingly.

**Find your inner strength.**

If you are overwhelmed by pain and think you can't do anything more, keep fighting. Continue to search for answers to all your questions. And if you can't find them, find a reason to keep looking. Because this is life - get up, move forward, fight, learn from mistakes, listen to your emotions and feel them.

Maybe you can't find the will today, but who knows what will happen tomorrow? Every day is a story that is yet to be written. Although sometimes you can't decide how it should end, you can still choose how it should start.

Carry on! Breathe in, fill your lungs, jump and fly. If you have to go back a little, recharge your batteries, improve your wings and gather strength from everything you have learned. And when you're done, dare the jump. Don't stop fighting because you have all the power and resources you need to take the path ahead of you. You have to find her in yourself.

But don't forget to allow **yourself a few days of being alone**. Make way for grief and fear. You have to experience these negative emotions to get up again and reach your full potential.

**You are not alone**

Don't lose hope. Continue working until you find the resources in you. Trust in your potential.

If you still feel weak, if the pain has subsided, then don't worry. You are not alone.

Find someone with whom you can relax, someone who can be a refuge for you. They will help you get back on your feet and find the strength to go further. It requires bravery to ask for and accept assistance.

If you need it, let yourself be helped, forget your fears and lean against the shoulders of your loved ones. Take their hand and release the load that pushes you down. You can do it!

If **you dream of it, believe in it, and act accordingly, you get closer and closer to your goal.**

Don't forget that there is no end without a new beginning, no light without darkness. You can't get up if you haven't fallen. You can't find strength or will if you don't look for it. Contrasts can make you grow if you find the center that balances them.

So keep going - find the strength, fight and get the most out of yourself. Get up, tap the dust and carry on because it's worth it.

**Don't forget that life goes on, time passes, and you write your own story.** You have the strength in you, so don't give up.

# CHAPTER 17

# KINDNESS

Kindness is the language that the deaf can hear, and the blind can see." Twain

The world revolves around kindness. Being good to ourselves helps us feel fantastic, and being kind to others makes us feel even better.

**Kindness is power, and love is kindness.**

Each of us possesses the ability to make another person feel good or bad. Every waking hour, we have a choice. We can generate a pleasant current experience by being aware of and drawing on positive temporal views (past positive instead of past negative, future positive instead of future fatalistic) experiences. Whether it's flashing a grin or complement to the person behind the counter or being unpleasant, whether it's assisting someone in need, such as an older person attempting to retrieve a product off a shelf at the grocery store, or simply going by.

We can release tension, make someone feel good about themselves, and make them realize, "It is good in the world." We can also do the polar opposite.

Being kind is an investment in the other person's and, ultimately, your own brighter, more optimistic future. It's a reflection of your goodness, your kindness.

Kindness is not only one of the most significant virtues and qualities we can have, but it also brings together several other virtues such as patience, tolerance, compassion, gratitude, and unconditional love.

We not only become kinder when we exercise kindness, but we also develop the virtues that come with it.

We've all performed an act of kindness, whether it was unintentional or intended.

We gave our spouse, family member, or friend a gift, and we aided someone in need. We've all experienced the incredible and powerful feeling of doing an act of kindness and seeing it have a positive ripple effect.

**So, Why Is Kindness The Key To Happiness And Success?**

Ask yourself, "What impact am I having right now, and how can I add value to the world?"

There are a few ways we may make a positive difference, and one of the most effective is through compassion. On the other hand, genuine kindness is what raises us, inspires, encourages, and drives us to do more for ourselves and others. Because kindness is the path to discovering and achieving our purpose, our purpose is the gateway to pleasure and success!

It's crucial to remember that, while we all want to be truly happy and prosperous, we're all always involved in relationships. In truth, our relationship, how we treat one another, how we communicate, and what we do for one another determine humanity's progress.

Like any other body function, we understand that humanity is a collective function like an organism, relying on all organs, body functions, and different processes to come together as a unit to do magical things.

Like any other body function, we also understand that we must fulfill our purpose and give whatever gift we have into the world to contribute to something more significant as a collective.

And, like cells, we need to communicate effectively, which means sharing with kindness, being kind, treating ourselves and others with respect, making an effort to understand the other person, and acting with empathy and compassion, especially when we know it will have a significant positive impact on a person or group of people.

## Kindness Is the Key to Happiness and Success for this reason.

We open ourselves up to chances that will enrich our lives emotionally, physically, and spiritually by discovering our purpose, giving back, doing good, and sharing our gift with the world.

That means being able to inspire others by our work or just by our energy and character. This causes a good ripple effect and understanding how we, as a tiny cell in a grand living organism, can balance and change the status of something as vast as a collective population.

Nothing beats seeing change happen right in front of our eyes because we choose to be kind, caring, and loving.

Not to mention that acts of kindness can significantly positively impact our mental and physical well-being. We learn to enjoy what we do, achieve, practice it and be kind to ourselves and our bodies. Furthermore, just as being nice to ourselves may entirely transform our perceptions of ourselves and our lives, being kind to others has the potential to completely change someone else's world, clean them up, restore their faith, and encourage them to alter their lives!

Know that a small act of kindness on our part can make a significant difference in someone's life is a huge success that fills our hearts with joy and satisfaction right away!

Why not try practicing kindness instead of battling, competing, criticizing, and being unpleasant on your way to "success"? Whether you're having trouble with it, being surrounded by negative individuals, or being naturally kind, you want to improve your kindness.

**Why wait?**

The relevance of time and time perspective in our life

Our time perspective—how we see the past, present, and future—has a significant impact on our life, yet few people realize it. In reality, we rarely think about time until it starts to run out.

You've experienced the nervous, overwhelming feeling that comes with being late for an appointment, losing track of time and forgetting to pick up the kids after school, or piling one more item onto an already overflowing to-do list and feeling anxious and "pressed" for time to complete even one item on the list. When this happens, what is going on inside of us?

Apart from the apparent lack of time, we are most likely subconsciously reliving a previous unfavorable incident in which we were late and had to pay the sometimes fatal repercussions. We may also feel a lot of present fatalism—the sensation of "I screwed up!"—as well as future negative—"I'm going to get myself in so much trouble if I don't watch it!"

Our time perspectives influence how we see ourselves, others, and the world around us. They can also affect how we act in certain situations. For example, you may believe you have plenty of time one day and decide to let someone into your lane of traffic.

On another day, you might be late, and those few seconds it would take to let someone in ahead of you feel a bit too valuable, so you rush through and don't let them in.

*Consider this: if you're already running late, do a few seconds matter?*

**Consider purchasing a VIRTU Kindness bracelet.**

The bracelet was made to encourage you to be nice to all living things, including yourself. This tool, a unique and unusual fashion piece, adds a special touch not only to yours suit, causal dress, and style but also to your personality. So choose your favorite and help VIRTU in making compassion hip!

# CHAPTER 18

# LOVING SOMEONE VS BEING IN LOVE

You've got butterflies in your tummy and are just looking at each other? Then the situation is clear: you have a huge crush on each other! There's a sense of romance in the air. But, as psychologists all around the world remind you, there is a distinction to be made between being in love and loving someone!

Indeed Adore is a beautiful thing, and there is plenty to love in this world. When life gets tough, love keeps us going and gives us a reason to get out of bed in the morning when we'd rather stay in bed. Love is a fundamental human need. Love is something we both desire to give and receive.

**What exactly is love?**

For such a complicated emotion, a simple query is all that is required. Although love is a powerful emotion, there is a distinction between loving someone and being in love.

Many individuals realize and appreciate the distinction between being loved and being in love, but describing the distinct experiences can be difficult.

Someone You Love

You can love a lot of people at the same time. We adore our loved ones, including our family, friends, and pets. To love someone is to care for them genuinely. You are concerned about their well-being, happiness and wish for the best for them.

When you love someone, they are significant in ways other than romantic. If you love someone but aren't in love with them, you're unlikely to feel passion or desire for them. It is a choice to love someone. We chose to love and have our family and friends in our lives.

**Being in a Relationship**

When you're entirely in love with someone, they have a hold on your heart like no other. When you are in love with someone, you care about their happiness and well-being in the same way that you do when you love them, but other sensations come with being in love.

When you're in love with someone, you want to bring them joy and happiness, but they're also a significant source of your joy and happiness. It can feel as if falling in love and being in love with someone is an irresistible force. It isn't something you make a conscious decision to do; it just happens.

Being in love with someone is a fantastic emotional experience. It's not just about how you feel about them when you're in love; it's also about how they make you think. Seeing, touching, and tasting the person you love can make you feel completely euphoric.

## The Difference between Love and Being in Love

What Is the Difference Between Being in Love and Loving Someone?

Though the emotions of loving and being in love with someone are similar, they are also vastly different.

In all honesty, while I'm giving you a definition to distinguish the two if you ever have a question about love versus in love, you'll probably know the answer instinctively.

The term "love" is frequently employed in such a casual manner that it appears to dilute its genuine meaning. It's a big deal to love someone. It's a big deal to fall in love with someone.

How do you feel about love and being in love? Have you ever been perplexed or torn about how you feel about someone? Have you ever experienced falling out of love with someone but still caring profoundly for them?

It's impossible to change your mind about who you love. That's one of the most challenging aspects of being in love: it's irrefutable.

# CHAPTER 19

# LOYALTY

Have you ever considered which is more important to you: love or loyalty?

Until lately, I hadn't.

When asked to pick between the two, the majority of the people I met chose loyalty. In many cases, they say this without any hesitation.

**How can you have one without the other**, was my first thinking.

But, if I had to pick between love and loyalty, which would I choose?

**The word "loyalty" means "true allegiance." So, what does this mean in terms of a relationship?**

In a relationship, having loyalty is knowing that your partner will always have your back and will be there for you no matter what. This provides the steadiness and solid foundation that any relationship needs to last the distance.

Respect, communication, affection, closeness, vulnerability, and compassion are some of the core elements of loyalty.

Loyalty entails a commitment to your partner, as well as the relationship and each other. To understand that you are wholly devoted to one another and that every action you make must be weighed against how it will affect your spouse and your relationship.

Loyalty is lovely alchemy of trustworthiness and respect. It's the wisdom that comes from understanding that all relationships have ups and downs, good and bad times. Will you simply throw in the towel if things get too complicated? Do you choose to roll up your sleeves and figure out how to enhance your relationship and be there for your partner, or do you do the latter? The key to reliability is knowing that you can always count on each other to have your backs, no matter what.

Making your partner, your best friend is what loyalty is all about. You're entirely dedicated to them and on their side. You don't have to give your consent all of the time, but you don't have to hold each other captive by making the other person incorrect.

This is the individual with whom you wish to spend the most of your time. While it's OK to have various hobbies and interests, you should call your partner first when you have good news.

They are also the first people you should contact if you require assistance.

Loyalty is defined as a desire to see your spouse and relationship succeed. Your relationship with your partner is involved in everything you do, everything you say, and everything you are. You're set on becoming a happy couple who can live out your fairy tale love story together.

You are your partner's biggest supporter, and you want them to be the best version of themselves so that they can encourage you to be the best version of yourself, making you the happiest couple, you know!

## How to Build Loyalty in Your Relationship

While we've covered some of the most popular ways to demonstrate devotion in a relationship, everyone is unique and has distinct ideas and values.

To develop a long-lasting relationship, you must first grasp what trust and loyalty mean to your partner and be on the same page.

Here are a few tips to build loyalty in your relationship today.

**Promises and secrets must be kept**

Honor your vows to one another, and don't keep secrets from one another.

**Leave your judgment at the door.**

Make sure to treat each other with respect and not pass judgment on your disagreements. Even if you don't understand why certain things are essential to your partner, what matters is that they are important to them.

**Don't Be Afraid to Show Your Vulnerability**.

Building loyalty and trust in a partnership requires honesty and openness. There are numerous advantages to being vulnerable. Accepting and Embracing Yourself (Flaws and All)

**Be Forgiving When you live your truth, your spouse will feel more at ease living theirs.**

To create and keep loyalty, forgiveness is necessary. We all make errors, and it's crucial to be quick to forgive. Holding grudges over past misdeeds will only cause the relationship to deteriorate.

Letting go of the hurt, embracing the apology, and forging on establishes a foundation of truth and love in the relationship.

Understanding that we are human, that we make mistakes, and that our partner would accept us as we are is essential to building trust and commitment.

**Commit to improving yourself.**

Personal development not only helps you become a better person, but it also helps you strengthen your relationship. It's critical to develop as individuals as well as a pair.

As they say on airplanes, put your oxygen mask on first before helping others. We can't be fully and completely present for our partners if we aren't taking care of ourselves. As a result, a more vital link is formed.

The necessity of loyalty, as well as continuing to build on it, is critical for a relationship to not only survive but to grow.

We all want to be safe and secure in a committed relationship that brings out our most exemplary traits as individuals and couples. It's because of this warmth, comfort, and deep knowing that our bond and devotion can withstand any difficulty.

# CHAPTER 20

# GRATITUDE

Learning more gratitude is not only the noblest way to more happiness and satisfaction. To become more grateful is the perfect antidote to frustration, envy, and anger.

Gratitude is what we long for ourselves most: for recognition and appreciation for what has been done, a simple "thank you" for a good, generous act. Writers, philosophers, and grandmothers rightly regularly urge us to be grateful: It is an essential key to success and fulfilling life.

**Why is gratitude so vital, and how can you learn to express it?**

Gratitude is more than a "thank you" because someone has done us a favor. Being grateful is an attitude. An attitude to life. Gratitude is the feeling of wonder, being grateful, and celebrating life, says Robert Emmons. Jean-

Baptiste Massillon says: "Gratitude is the memory of the heart."

Even the joy of the little things in life has been proven to lead to more happiness. Those who establish a grateful attitude in their lives give themselves time to pause, mentally rest, and reflect.

**Gratitude is like breathing deeply.** We look at our lives and recognize its true wealth.

Consider what you have to be thankful for. In the following list, you will undoubtedly find more than what we have...

**What we can be (more) grateful for**

- Your health.
- Our partner and a stable relationship.
- (Healthy) children.
- Our friends.
- A cozy home.
- The grace to be born in a free and peaceful country.

The list is endless

Not every day is pleasant, but every day has something satisfying; all you have to do is acknowledge it (want to). Gratitude can change our lives: those who are grateful experience a deep sense of happiness, satisfaction, and joy not only in the short term. It becomes a state over time. The generally good basic mood that generates gratitude leads to a so-called "broaden-and-built effect," this means that people who live gratefully have more and more positive effects.

We value our lives more again. Especially the small things.

- We BECOME more confident.
- We radiate more satisfaction and thus have a more pleasing effect on others.
- We can better resist temptations because we need less.
- We react to changes with less stress.
- We have fewer fears.
- We recognize more opportunities and possibilities.
- We are becoming more relaxed towards crises and can manage them faster.

- We are becoming more resilient.
- We strengthen our well-being and self-esteem.
- We pave the way for a fulfilling life.

## Lack of gratitude: ungratefulness is a career killer

Without gratitude, on the other hand, a defective view often develops life - it consists above all of the gaps, missing, and emptiness. Those who perceive themselves and their environment in this way can only become dissatisfied, jealous, and unhappy.

The grass next door is always greener for these people, the sky next door is bluer, and the neighbor's car is more beautiful anyway. Such ungratefulness is dangerous!

According to Goethe, grateful people are capable. History proves him correct: It was not those who had a lot who were successful, but the grateful. Or, as another quote says: "Not the lucky ones are grateful. It is the grateful ones who are happy.

Nobody will be thankful for future successes if he cannot already be with current ones.

Moreover: ungratefulness can mutate into a career killer. Ungrateful is a lack of recognition and lack of gratitude for support. For example, by sticking success to their lapel and concealing that others were involved. Forgetfulness, however, weighs even heavier. Nobody expects an immediate return for a favor but remember, one hand wash the other.

## Learn gratitude: 5 tips

Gratitude is like a muscle: If it is not trained regularly. We, humans, seldom appreciate what we have.

We become blind to existing wealth and take it for granted. This makes the positive effect of gratitude evaporate.

A classic habituation effect. This makes it all the more important to keep pushing yourself aware of what we can and should be grateful for. But how can gratitude be learned and strengthened?

There are numerous recommendations and tips for this. I present the five most ingenious here:

**The 5-finger method: A thank you with every finger.**

If you are dissatisfied with life or need a motivational kick, just count your fingers and remember beautiful, satisfying, and encouraging things in your life." For example:

**Thumbs (up):** Name something you are proud of. Be aware of your strengths and talents - and be proud of yourself.

**Index finger:** Point to something beautiful in nature. Discover something in your environment that inspires and inspires you.

**Middle finger:** Name one thing you have done for another person and what you feel good for. Think about who you can repeat this with—for example, today.

**Ring finger:** Remember a time and a person you love or loved from the bottom of your heart as well as other people for whom you have heartfelt feelings.

**Little finger:** Name one thing for which you are deeply grateful in your life.

The hand idea has charm because, firstly, it is catchy, and secondly, it can be repeated at any time.

If you always want to have the whole cake for yourself, you only get a stomach ache from it. On the other hand, the unselfish act and a "thank you," on the other hand, pay off in the long term.

**Get a gratitude diary.**

This is a variant of the success diary - only you answer the question daily: "What am I grateful for today?" This exercise aims to make yourself aware of how well you are doing and sharpen the senses for what it is worth being grateful for using a positive review of the day.

The effect is that in the future, we will enjoy the relationships and experiences in everyday life more and experience them more consciously - a friendly word, a gifted smile, a beautiful sunset.

It is recommended to maintain the gratitude diary in the form of an evening ritual. But you can also write this as part of your morning routine.

# CHAPTER 21

# GIVING BACK

Do you remember how good it feels to assist an elderly neighbor with shoveling their driveway after a storm?

What about helping the mom with her hands full at the grocery store in carrying her cart to her car? When was the last time you gave your hard-earned money to a cause you truly believe in and care about?

Giving back to the community has a multiplier effect beyond the persons or organizations you've generously assisted with your time or money.

## The Feelings of Charity - The Power of Giving

Researchers compared the psychological effects of those who provided similar or equal gifts to others vs. receiving those same gifts over some time in two studies published in 2018—according to the findings, giving to a person or charity triggered a more prolonged, more resonant feeling of enjoyment than receiving the same or similar present themselves.

We frequently hear suggestions like "You need a change!" or "Time to try something new!" when we are suffering feelings of dissatisfaction or despair.

We believe that change and new experiences are essential to our brains, which is why we seek out endorphin-releasing activities or tangible goods that can make us feel better. However, the power of giving may be an excellent method to navigate a sea of uncertainty and find ways to make us feel better, more confident, and cherished.

People who choose to contribute their earnings or "gifts" to a charity regardless of outside influence derived a delight they got from being charitable motivated them to give despite the cloak of anonymity at their fingertips.

**There Isn't Such a Thing as a Random Act of Kindness - What Exactly Is Giving Back?**

The beauty of giving comes down to a simple concept. Participants in the trials mentioned above made little charity offerings, sometimes less than $5 each day.

The donation was not made from their bank account in these instances.

The parameters of these studies, on the other hand, allowed them to keep some of the money they would otherwise give away, allowing them to prioritize giving to charity over personal gain.

When you consider the broad psychology driving the impact of giving back, you might ask if it matters how you donate or how much you can give.

The vast majority of the responses to the primary research painted a fairly clear picture for us: no quantity of your valuable time and no cash amount of your donation is too big or small. These same sentiments of enjoyment can be achieved by donating whatever money or time you have available.

Choosing a cause or community to assist with your charity action means a lot for a good reason, and it may help your sense of self-worth and value take you to a higher level of confidence and pleasure, which is a win-win situation for everyone!

You might be wondering if it matters how you donate or how much you can offer. The vast majority of the responses to the primary research painted a fairly clear picture for me. No quantity of your valuable time and no cash amount of your donation is too big or small.

These same sentiments of enjoyment can be achieved by donating whatever money or time you have available.

Choosing a cause or community to assist with your charity action means a lot for a good reason, and it may help your sense of self-worth and value take you to a higher level of confidence and pleasure, which is a win-win situation for everyone!

# CHAPTER 22

# UNDERSTANDING

Couples unite because they share a common belief in happiness. Couples remain together because they believe they can make it work. Love, security, and trust are all qualities that people in partnerships crave.

I believe there is a way to construct a fantastic relationship, but you can't do it unless you fully understand your own and your partner's inner feelings.

Understanding is a fundamental component of a successful and happy relationship. Every relationship should aim to accept the other as they are and love them unreservedly.

Why can't he/she grasp what I'm saying? Isn't he/she aware of how important this is to me? Why don't they seem to care about my needs?

**Are you aware of this?**

Everyone wants a spouse who understands them. Expecting anything from someone else, on the other hand, implies that you are also willing to do it yourself. So here's the question: are you indeed prepared to meet your spouse with complete understanding?

Of course, your personal needs come first, but they can be reconciled with those of your spouse without either of you having to take a step back.

You don't have to agree on all of the time. It is sufficient to perceive each other as you are rather than as you wish. Many people spend a lot of time (and energy) trying to persuade their partner to think the same way they do.

Stop immediately if you want to develop a meaningful bond.

What is the difference between understanding and comprehension?

You can only comprehend anything if you have personally experienced it. Everyone has a distinct perspective on the experience, but it is much easier to understand emotionally.

In all other circumstances, we require comprehension. Understanding is especially vital when we don't understand the other person or hi point of view.

It is also unimportant that we fully comprehend one other. What is at stake is to presume that things are as they are. We don't have to understand everything if we know each other; we can accept it.

Understanding frequently extends beyond the intellect. - Ebner-Eschenbach, Marie

**How does one come to understand something?**

You don't have to accept or even approve every conduct just because you understand it. Instead, it means being willing to look at how the other is doing with curiosity and courage.

Examine his emotions and learn about his desires, needs, thoughts, and fantasies. And it's crucial that you let this inner world of your partner exist, that you leave it alone and don't try to eliminate, reject, repress, or devalue it.

Everything can simply be there, open and value-free, and will be accepted as is. This has an impact on both you and your relationship. Those who lack this will send a message to their spouse that something is wrong with them. That can't be his feelings.

You wish to manage, control, and remove the other person's "bad" conduct. But there is a fight back. Backpressure is created when pressure is applied, and such an approach invariably results in conflict. If we don't feel understood, we either make a protective wall or go on the offensive. Both are ineffective in maintaining a good relationship.

Just because you comprehend something doesn't mean you agree with it.

We must listen to each other better and communicate more effectively if we wish to improve our comprehension of our partner's reality. Although we both speak the same language, our words frequently have different meanings. This is because we have all had different life experiences, all of which have influenced our language somehow. Take, for example, the word "love." When you speak this term, you immediately get a concrete idea, making you feel a certain way. That's how you define love.

We all feel the same thing, just in different ways. After all, we've all had different experiences with love that have impacted our perceptions of it. This awareness is crucial in a relationship since it can reduce or even eliminate disagreements.

**Is it possible to learn to understand?**

Of course, comprehension is something that can be learned. Some people are already more emphatic than others in terms of personality type, but we may all have it if we want to. It's a process to which we can devote some time. Any conflict with our spouse provides an opportunity for us to practice. It doesn't always work out right away, and we'll have to deal with headwinds as well. But our will is decisive, and we should have it when the relationship is important to us.

I've produced a list of five recommendations to help you get started. Assist you in training and improving your comprehension...

1) Acknowledgement

Acceptance is the fundamental building component of comprehension—acceptance that we are all self-contained individuals with differing perspectives and needs.

2) Attractiveness

Taking an interest in something is also a step toward understanding. Open-ended questions show the other that his needs and well-being are important to us.

3) Generosity

When we empathize with our partners, we get as close to each other on an emotional level as possible. Empathy can be crucial, especially in instances where people's viewpoints are opposed.

4) Making concessions

A popular approach is to make a compromise. When we compromise, we frequently only perceive the things we appear to have to "give up." It can feel delightful if we focus on unity and joint progress.

5) Individual accountability

It is critical to take responsibility for oneself, as it is with everything else in life. We've compiled a list of five suggestions to assist you. With your training and comprehension.., I can contribute to the conversation. My boyfriend is completely unaware of how I'm feeling. It is my responsibility to convey this information.

# CHAPTER 23

# EXPRESS GRATITUDE IN YOUR RELATIONSHIPS

*There will be no end if you do what you did at the start of a relationship.*

Gratitude strengthens the bond between two people.

When we stop appreciating each other, we suffocate the fire of love. We make each other feel important by expressing our gratitude and acknowledging each other's contributions. Gratitude is the most potent love enhancer there is.

**What exactly is gratitude?**

As you would see in previous chapters gratitude is made up of various elements. On the one hand, it's the pure joy of receiving a gift, which we've mastered since childhood. It's also the ability to recognize the donor's good intentions and thank them with words or a similarly generous gesture.

The most profound form of gratitude is a humble attitude toward all of life. Accept everything for what it is while also seeing it as a gift. This type of gratitude is more of a decision than a feeling. It allows us to focus on what we have rather than what we lack. It's a subtle sensation that has a long-lasting positive impact on our overall well-being.

We are not immediately content, but we are pleased in the long run. Over time, this sustained well-being transforms into satisfaction, making us feel like we're living a happy life.

This is true only if we make gratitude a fundamental attitude that is so consistent that it is almost a personality trait. It becomes a permanent conscious attitude rather than a situational practice at some point.

Although gratitude has been scientifically proven, this does not mean that those who are grateful must always be happy. You can have a grateful attitude while also allowing negative emotions to exist. The crucial difference is that you gratefully acknowledge and apply your learning task even under challenging situations. Not only does he dwell on the negative and remain in pain, but he also sees the positive side of things.

**What role does thankfulness play in a partnership??**

We shower each other with gratitude at the start of a relationship. "Thank you for being there," or "Thank you for being so wonderful," or "Thank you for always being there for me," or "Thank you for always being there for me."." But, behind all of these statements, there isn't a genuine sense of gratitude for the other. It's simply your relief to have a partner by our side at long last.

This ostensibly selfish behavior is entirely normal and not at all repulsive.

We all yearn for deep attachment to another person, and we feel deeply fulfilled once we believe we have achieved it. Or, at the very least, to have taken a significant step forward in his strategy.

We lose this grateful relationship over time and in regular life, and at some point, we regard each other as a given. This is not only unfortunate, but it is also detrimental to the relationship. Gratitude, after all, is not just a lovely gesture; it also strengthens the bond between two people.

When we express gratitude to someone, we are naturally compelled to keep in touch with them. This is, of course, very advantageous in long-term relationships. If both partners make it a point to be grateful to each other at all times, they will immediately contribute to the relationship's longevity.

We all want to be acknowledged, especially by the people who matter the most to us. And thanks are nothing more than a form of acknowledgment. The significant part is that we are eager to reciprocate by giving our partner the same sensation as soon as we receive them. "Like you to me, so I to you" takes on a whole new and far more positive meaning than we typically associate with it.

Gratitude offers far more benefits than simply "maintaining" a connection. After all, it isn't just about keeping the relationship alive but also about how well it is doing. Couples that practice thankfulness are happier feel closer to one another, and have stronger bonds.

Gratitude also contributes to a sense of security. This is crucial because it is one of the most basic human needs and a fundamental relationship-building element. As a result, the partners feel more at ease, and their readiness to open up to one another grows. This sense of comfort in the relationship allows you to express your demands more clearly, which is essential for a happy and satisfying partnership.

Gratitude encourages us to spend more time with each other and fosters a sense of belonging and trust on both sides.

**In a relationship, how does gratitude work?**

In a relationship, gratitude includes not only appreciating what your partner does for you but also loving them for who they are. Of course, we can see it right now.

This is where mindfulness enters the picture. I can admire this individual purely because of who they are if I consciously realize who's is by my side.

Gratitude becomes the key to happiness if couples succeed. There is little severe potential for conflict if you focus on all of your partner's positive attributes and characteristics. Of course, it's not about constantly chatting to your partner, but we don't have to condemn each other for everything. On the other hand, we can emphasize mutual appreciation and treat one another with thanks.

**What is the best way to express and appreciate gratitude?**

Being openly grateful is, in fact, complex. Because we frequently express emotions. Gratitude makes us vulnerable. So, if you've never really learned to be appreciative, you could find this difficult at first. But, as with everything else in life, practice pays off.

The lovely thing is that when we thank our partners, we get direct and very significant feedback. So it could feel awkward and bumpy at first, but the result will always be satisfying – guaranteed!

The assumption of thankfulness is not to be overlooked. It necessitates a high level of self-esteem. After all, we all have an inner voice that likes to cast doubt on deep appreciation and acclaim.

We can purposely drown them out. We are deserving of respect and gratitude. And it's not just because we've done something extraordinary; it's also because of ourselves. It's also critical that we make our partners aware of our acceptance. Because an unappreciated thank you is useless.

**Gratitude is thus expressed in the following steps:**

**The first is to recognize it**. The second is to tell them to the others through words or gestures. The assumption is the third point to consider.

As a result, both spouses benefit from practicing thankfulness.

Everyone may practice being appreciative straightforwardly and openly and accepting others in love.

Thanking someone develops something. It communicates an emotion that underpins everything positive in the relationship.

**What do you have to thank your partner for?**

Gratitude has no limits. You can express your appreciation for your lover in whatever way you wish. It's critical to realize that genuine appreciation entails much more than simply saying "thank you." True thankfulness carries a unique message that transcends words.

Sometimes, more than anything else, how we express thanks is far more critical than what we say. As a result, we should always communicate with them exactly as we feel them. Both vocally and nonverbally, this can occur. A warm hug, for example, might offer far more gratitude than lovely words.

To cultivate thankfulness, it's helpful to approach ordinary relationship life with a fresh perspective. Simply pay attention to what your partner does, as well as why and how he/she does it. After all, it is often the motive behind the deeds that touches our emotions, not the deeds themselves.

And, because thoughts are transient, it's a good idea to jot down a quick letter or express your gratitude to your partner immediately.

"**Gratitude entails appreciating the unique in everyday life.**"

It can be the most insignificant and insignificant things for which we are grateful to our beloved.

A particular sensation is triggered by a loving gesture, an honest word, or even simply a thought.

# CHAPTER 24

# FORGIVENESS

*"We release a prisoner when we forgive someone, only to learn that we were the prisoner!"*

*Carrie ten Boom.*

## What does forgiveness mean?

**Forgiveness** is a mental reaction to misconduct that has taken place. It is independent of guilt or recognition of responsibility. For me, forgiveness means first and foremost that one moves from the role of victim to the actor's part.

Forgiveness is often a lengthy process that should not result in you forgetting a horrible event. You just release it from your heart.

For me, I go so far as to say that forgiveness does not mean forgiveness, especially if it was something awful that happened to you.

## Does it have consequences for me if I can't forgive?

First of all, we refrain from the visible and noticeable consequences of the injury. Yes, it has effects. Because it is always there, this tiny sting of damage and sometimes more, sometimes less, makes it's way and brings the experience back to light. You can't lock. The bad thing about it is that you are reminded, again and again, questioned again and sad.

The event is always present and gains power over you. But that's not right - you should decide what's good for you and not let such an event take control. Therefore: Yes, it has consequences.

## How do I forgive now?

Forgiven is a trip. To learn it too. But it makes you lighter, more liberated, and takes away the attribute' victim.' You're getting active.

Forgiveness can occur without the apology and presence of the 'perpetrator' because we sometimes wait in vain for them, and it is sometimes doubtful whether it is meant seriously. Forgiveness only happens with and in yourself - without the intervention of others.

It is also a little comparable to letting go. Your victim role is negated. You have to tell yourself: I forgive ABC for what they did. Loud in front of yourself. This does not, however, indicate that you are a nasty person, approves of the situation. You just let it go.

I believe that such a thing is not always easy; I know that. But it makes you easier afterward and gives you back control.

It also does not mean that you must or can face the person in the future without value or carefree. Because this only works if this person has demonstrably changed their behavior or apologizes. But you can heal without the spite coming to the surface.

## **Forgiveness can also mean separation**.

If someone hurt you very much or hurt you, so much so that you no longer want to deal with this person, you should still try to forgive them for you.

Otherwise, this person will stick forever in your head and heart, and when you see them you feel bad, experience the past over and over again.

So if a situation is so bad or escalated that you can't or don't want to be with the person anymore, then forgive them and let them move on.

Then you are more accessible and feel freer because you have removed this slight poisonous sting from you and are more open again.

## Why do we need forgiveness?

Forgiveness has a lot to do with emotional intelligence. We need them to put ourselves back in the role of the actor. For if you do not forgive, you are and will remain an (unjustified) victim. You act and react afterward and thus take away your freedom. You can't want that.

Besides, we don't want to make a murder pit out of our hearts, and we want to enjoy this one life we have.

## What happens after forgiveness?

There are very different scenarios:

- You have the impression that the one who hurt you regrets it and changes their behavior (which is, of course, the happy ending solution). Then you resume your relationship.
- You notice how you can move and give up more freely again because you have clarified the matter for yourself.
- You know that they will continue to be like this (and always been so) and draw a line under the whole thing. This is the most unpleasant but sometimes necessary solution. And nevertheless, you are free because you could forgive.

The consequence of forgiveness should always serve your relief and also freedom. Therefore practice forgiving. As I said, this is possible without personal contact, and it helps you to regain old strength.

Although I am well aware that it is not always easy.

## The power of forgiveness gives you control over your feeling.

Isn't it great if you can say (regardless of the **consequences** you'll draw): I forgive you, and then you go, and the sting is removed without a doctor's visit?

As I said, it's not always that easy, and you have to practice it, but it's excellent at the end of the journey to forgiveness to know that no one has control and power over you and your feelings.

Fortunately, it is never too soon to forgive someone. But why is forgiveness often so difficult? Why is it easier for us in some relationships and more complex in others? Does award also mean forgotten? Can I also demand forgiveness?

I would like us to take a closer look at some of the questions below.

### Why is forgiveness so difficult?

Just as a physical injury hurts, an internal injury also hurts. If the other insults expose, slanders me, criticizes me, or do not pay the hoped-for attention, there is no apparent injury, and the inner pain is still present. Inside it is bubbling. I'm thinking about how I can react, take revenge or defend myself. Anger, and maybe even hatred are spreading.

Forgiveness is out of the question at this moment. It's about me, about my hurt honor, my hurt pride, maybe also about self-pity.

What has happened contradicts my sense of justice and may destroy my reputation. And that's precisely why forgiveness is so difficult for me because I look at myself as I am at the center of attention at that moment.

How can I respect the others higher than myself when I am in this inner prison and feed my "wrong" sensitivities?

Forgiveness costs me something at this moment. Because forgiveness now means that there may not be justice or that the damage cannot be undone or repaired. I have to let go of something. I have to cope with a loss and give up power, which I may have taken over through the role of victim.

But what is the price if I don't forgive? Resentment and anger take up space in me. The other has power over me and my negative emotions. Is it worth it? Wouldn't it be better to jump over my own shadow now, be humble and merciful to forgive the other?

In the same way, as we pray the Lord's Prayer - "And forgive us our guilt, just as we forgive our culprits" - I would like to imitate God's character, be merciful to my fellow human beings, and live this in word and deed. But of course, this does not go from one minute to the next but takes time and a new perspective.

## Steps to forgiveness

Over time, I have found a way for myself to deal with such situations. This is not a scheme that I always apply in a particular form. But it helps to bring structure into your thoughts and to come down emotionally.

As soon as the emotional chaos has subsided, I realize the pain and admit that it hit me, and it hurt. Whether the other did it on purpose or accidentally, it broke me, and I can admit that.

**Allow the existing anger**. This helps me to gain distance. I don't want to be broken or controlled by the other. I decide to leave the passive victim role and take the active part. I objectively review the process and try to separate the act from the perpetrator.

What might my counterpart have thought? What did they mean by it? What situation were they in right now? Did they perhaps only pass on their injuries to me? Did they hit my sensitive side without intention and isn't even aware of it? If someone else had acted like this, would the effect on me have been the same?

I try to understand what happened so that I can understand myself.

Only then can I free myself from the negative feelings in me through the injury and give them to God in prayer. This means that I deliberately decide to forgive and pray that God will cause this forgiveness in me. I pray for the other. This allows me to let it go so that it no longer has power over me.

In the final step, **I consider how I can turn this injury into pearls.** Every conflict, every injury takes me a step further on my path, and I learn new things about myself. The pearl also grows in the wound of oysters - so I can also discover the pearl in my injury.

## Forgiveness does not mean forgetting.

Forgiveness does not imply that I must forget everything and wrap myself around the other's neck as if nothing had occurred. Forgiveness means letting go, giving up. I leave the hurt with the other person. Then I can be friendly and familiar with them again.

Maybe I still need distance to protect myself, but I am no longer bound to the other. The wound is washed, but it still needs some time to heal. God can make a complete restoration of the relationship possible in due course - I can pray for this, and I can trust in it.

In addition, I can learn from every person who hurt me, which things are hurtful. I am probably hurt by precisely the behavior that also harms others. As a result, I'm more aware of how I shouldn't treat others.

I recognize true forgiveness because the relationship with the person who hurt me does not change. I don't avoid them. If I do, I haven't forgiven them. If the other avoids me even though I have reconciled with them, that's their business. Then I try to approach him with patience. But I can't demand his forgiveness.

# CHAPTER 25

# TRUST YOUR INSTINCT

Learning to trust your intuition, sometimes known as your gut, can help you stay safe. Your instincts can lead you in the right direction and aid in the development of confidence and resilience.

On several occasions, my gut instinct has rescued me. It has also helped me make wise career decisions and other significant life decisions. I'm also aware of times when I've gone against my instincts and later regretted it, wondering why I didn't listen to that invaluable internal voice we all possess.

In this section, we'll look at why and how you should listen to your gut, as well as some practical advice on getting the most out of your gut feeling.

**How to Pay Attention to Your Gut Feelings**

When making any major decision, it's critical to take a moment to listen carefully to yourself and your inner compass.

If you hear your voice say yes while silently screaming no within, my recommendation is to request some time to think or simply take a breath and pause before answering yes or no.

Use that time to take a deep breath, check-in with yourself, and respond in a manner that is true to who you are and what you want, rather than the one that always entails following the herd. Having the bravery not simply to follow the crowd involves trusting your instincts. It could be about being able to stand on your own two feet. Here's how you can perfect that skill and get the benefits.

**Pay attention to your body.**

When you're faced with a significant decision, your body provides you cues. In stressful conditions, we experience a variety of apparent and obvious symptoms.

Our bodies' reactions are often things we strive to disguise, such as blushing, speechless, or shaking. Wearing cosmetics, having a glass of wine or coffee to perk us up a little, or learning to control our anxiety are all things we may do to mask that physical reaction.

Paying attention to your body when you're experiencing worry, on the other hand, can teach you a lot and help you make better decisions. Some people will get a "gut" feeling of stomach ache or indigestion in an uncomfortable circumstance.

Examine what's going on here and what's going on beneath your body's reaction to the scenario. What can your instinct or reaction teach you? That can be a sign, and understanding it can help you learn about yourself, the circumstance, or other people. We often have the answers within us.

These days, I listen to my gut instincts.

I don't question it; I just do what it says.

Even when what comes my way is startling and unexpected, I remain open and intrigued as I learn what happens next along the route, trusting that it will take me to what I want or need. When it appears to be leading me in a direction, I don't believe I want to go, and it reminds me to reconsider the path I've chosen.

Following my intuition is a delicate way of going forward in my life, which is in sync with my rhythms and pace.

It's made me feel more connected to life, like if I'm being held by something bigger than myself, something that knows more about what I'm here to do than I do and will help me open and flow in that if I allow it.

I'm also more aware of myself these days and can better say YES or NO to whatever comes my way. My responses are based on what I can currently see to be correct or incorrect for me and how much energy I have available at any one time. I guess as a result of that, I've become less of a people pleaser! I'm saying NO, a lot more than I used to – hopefully gently and for the right reasons.

My intuitive living isn't without flaws. It may never be. I'm not always sure how I feel about things, and intuitive instincts can be hazy or perplexing at times. But as I continue to practice with awareness and reflection on how I felt, what I did or didn't do, and what happened afterward, it's becoming easier for me. It's all a part of the process and if I lose touch with my instincts, I'll be in big trouble. I'll work hard to re-establish it. As soon as possible!

**How to start trusting your gut instincts.**

I've listed seven principles that I've found helpful and continue to follow — I hope they'll be beneficial to you as well!

**1 Calm down, unwind and be still.**

You must be able to hear your intuition's voice to listen to it. This is tough to do when life is hectic, with a million things clamoring for your attention, and stress, high emotions, and jumbled ideas rife. Yourself, to relax and be quiet both inside and out, will aid you in noticing what your gut instinct is telling you

Can you put an end to even a couple of the things you're doing? Should you resolve disagreements or avoid them? Do you want to take your life at a more leisurely pace? Is it possible for you to consciously schedule time for rest? Do you prefer to process or discharge your negative emotions? How do you calm down and stop your thoughts from racing?

Choose anything that seems suitable for you, commit to it regularly, and see what occurs!

**2. Learn to be more mindful.**

You can learn to pay more attention to what's happening around you and within yourself. In the middle of a frenetic environment, meditation, for example, can help you quiet your thoughts and become still(er). Then mindfulness practices can assist you in tuning in to the world and yourself, focusing your attention mindfully, and practicing noticing things.

All of this will help you better 'hear' and identify the voice of your gut feeling from other impulses.

Rather than reacting reflexively just to get something done or off your back, you'll be able to perceive more clearly what's going on and sense your optimal answer.

**3. Try it on to see how it fits.**

This one is quite useful because I can't always tell whether something is good for me just by thinking about it. But when I test it out for real, I get a sense of how it feels, and then I know.

What is it about which you are unsure? What if you couldn't try it on for size?

(If you can't accomplish it in real life, you'll never be able to do it in the virtual world. you can go over the details of what it means to do it in your head.) What does it feel like to picture oneself performing this?)

In any case, take note of the following: How does it make you feel? What does your inner voice say about it?

**4 Inquire about information.**

When I discovered this, I was astounded: You can genuinely ask your intuition questions about things you don't understand.

Ask your intuitive knowledge, the wise part within you, "Should I be doing this?" Get still (maybe in meditation, or wandering alone in nature, or whichever method works for you) and ask: "Should I be doing this?" Then sit back and wait for your response.

It could manifest as a feeling YES or NO or as a forward (=YES) or backward (=NO) sway of your body. (For further information, see Using Your Body as a Pendulum.) Maybe you won't hear anything, but you'll sense or know what the proper answer is for you.

You can also inquire, "What does this mean?" or "How should I begin?" Or anything else that would assist you in determining the best course of action.

Don't overthink it, don't overanalyze it; simply wait for an answer. Allow it to rest if nothing comes up right away. If you're anything like me, you'll appreciate this. You might find that an answer emerges at an inopportune time!

**5 Pick an intelligent card.**

When I'm unsure about something or someone, I like to consult my three-card sets: energy cards, power animal cards, and wisdom cards. I recently added a fourth one, which contains cards with just one word on them, such as joy, commitment, reflection, faith, love, celebration, and so on.

Of course, you may like angel cards, tarot cards, Goddess cards, thoughts cards, image cards, color cards, or... whichever card set feels right in your core.

Cards can be consulted in various ways, but the most basic is to mix your card deck while thinking about the question, doubt, or misunderstanding you want to clear up. Then, face down, layout the cards. Allow your hand to move over the cards and notice where it wants to stop; then choose a card from that location.

Then consider what it reveals or says.

Would you interpret the meaning of the card literally, or should you interpret it figuratively as a story, an image, or a symbol that connects to your question?

What does that signify in terms of your current circumstance, your inquiry, and your perplexity? What ideas or responses does it elicit in you? Do you believe they're right or wrong?

**6 Keep an eye out for coincidences.**

Synchronicities - seemingly unconnected, extraordinary, even miraculous coincidences – have long been seen to have meaning and provide insight, as they correspond to our emotional states and inner experiences. Some feel these are winks and nods from the Universe, letting us know we're on the right track if we pay attention.

Did you notice that on certain days, you see the same sequence of numbers – say, 11:11 or 44:44 – in various unrelated places? People run across someone they haven't seen in twenty years, at random places at random times. If you want to learn more about synchronicity, the first step is to notice them. You might even feel compelled to write them down in a journal and observe them for a while.

**7: Believe that your inner wisdom is wiser than you realize.**

Decide that the next time you get a hunch, an inspiration, or a gut feeling about something or someone, you will simply pursue it, no questions asked.

Try performing it in a lighthearted and playful manner: Experiment with it, have some fun and see what happens.

Be grateful for every small thing that feels right to you and for every synchronicity you detect. Keep an eye on what happens. And don't be too concerned if nothing appears to be happening.

Continue to practice with an open mind, and you'll develop a stronger connection with your inner wisdom. It will become your friend, with whom you will contact frequently. You'll have a better sense of what's excellent or incorrect for you now that you have an inner compass to rely on.

With confidence, you might start making different decisions than previously. Observe how your confidence, well-being, and joy are developing as your life becomes more aligned with who you indeed are and how you're managing better with life's inevitable ups and downs!

Oh, and don't forget to appreciate this new direction in your life

# CHAPTER 26

# CONSISTENCY

"It's a simple and generous life rule that whatever you practice, you'll get better at it. Elizabeth Gilbert is a well-known author.

If we only show up once, nothing happens. Because we are always there for our children, they trust us, and we keep them secure. Day after day, our paychecks continue to arrive as long as we show up for work every day... even laundry is steady.

When we continuously engage with the people in our lives, we establish TRUST and connect.

That is why consistency is beneficial to MARKETING, creating and maintaining a marriage, parenting our children, caring for our bodies, and everything else in life. Walking for 10 minutes every day has better outcomes than walking 5 miles once a month.

So, what keeps us from being CONSISTENT in our day-to-day lives??

The key to CONSISTENCY is that it must be long-lasting. Meaning, whatever you do, you must do it consistently; else, it will not stick. CONSISTENCY is difficult, if not impossible, to maintain when we are not being genuine or doing the things we naturally like.

Consider the case of exercise. It's impossible to go to the gym consistently every week if you despise it; willpower can only get you so far. So, now that you know you need to exercise how about choosing something you enjoy doing? Do you have a basketball court in your driveway? Are you going for a walk with your dog? Do you like to dance in your kitchen? Do you want to go to the gym with a friend? Whatever it is, being consistent will be easier if you can create it in a way you enjoy.

So here's how it works:

**CONSISTENCY + LOVE**

Love what you do and do it regularly

I could contact you in other ways, but I like writing. I can express myself and share what I have to offer by writing. As a result, I chose something I ENJOY as the vehicle to connect with you CONSISTENTLY.

*Here's something to work on:*

What are some of the aspects of your life that you find challenging? Could you use some CONSISTENT effort?? Is it because of your health? What are your relationships like? Is this your company? Determine which one it is.

Consider this situation: what activity, if applied consistently, would make a difference?

What does that action have to do with what you naturally enjoy doing?

**How to Be Consistent In Whatever You Do In Life | 10 Laws of Consistency**

We all can be so much more than we are right now. We come up with so many excellent ideas and take significant initiatives for our growth and well-being throughout our lives, and we go to great lengths to get started and get things moving.

However, once the initial buzz has died down, staying steady and in the flow can be tricky. Eventually, we have to give up.

Let's face it, and most people struggle with consistency.

So many beautiful ideas and projects are buried in the dirt and never come to fruition. Because of a lack of consistency, many people who can achieve great things never do.

We frequently have many good ideas and thoughts, and we know what we "should" do to improve our lives' quality. If we could only be consistent in following some of our life's callings, our lives would be transformed beyond our wildest dreams.

We'll look at ten principles for being consistent in anything you do in this brief guide.

Whether you're looking for discipline and consistency in accomplishing your goals, being consistent in your start-up business, maintaining consistency in the habits you want to cultivate, or just being consistent in your life in general, you've come to the right place.

These ten rules will help you maintain consistency in any area you want to master.

I'm not going to tell you how important it is to plan, schedule, and set goals.

If you're reading this, chances are you've set some goals and are working toward them setting on some level, and you already know that creating goals and making plans to reach them isn't the real deal.

The true challenge is to stick to your plans and remain consistent with your efforts.

Being Consistent is a PRINCIPLE, period.

**COMMIT ONLY IF YOU ARE SURE YOU WANT TO DO IT.**

The majority of crucial things to consider before committing to something is whether you genuinely want to do it.

People frequently make decisions in the heat of the moment, and their decisions are based on the face value of objects. They don't take the time to think it through, which is why they don't know how much commitment it takes to achieve the desired results.

**Consider the following questions before committing to anything significant:**

Are you indeed prepared to confront the obstacles that will inevitably arise?

Are you prepared to put forth the effort? To study and develop all of the skills you'll need along the way??

Are you willing to set aside time for this, even if it means sacrificing other priorities?

First and foremost, are you sure this is what you want? Is this something you're doing on the spur of the moment? What is your true motivation for desiring this? Be truthful to yourself.

## ONE PRIMARY OBJECTIVE AT A TIME

Choose one thing and persist with it until it becomes a part of you. If you want to build a good habit, keep working on it. Don't try to create more than one habit at a time until the first one has become ingrained in your mind.

If you're working on a skill, concentrate on mastering that ONE skill.

If you're starting a business, don't pursue other ideas until you've put enough time and effort into the initial one. You can go on to other ideas after it's set up and running like a well-oiled machine.

In other words, don't take on more than you can handle.

Don't overcomplicate things. Make it SUSTAINABLE by keeping it simple.

When starting something new, a lot of people get caught up in the minute. They make things far more complicated than it needs to be.

Simplicity is the key to long-term sustainability.

Become too engrossed in the situation details in the beginning. It will be challenging to go on. It will be difficult to move on. It will be challenging to go on. While striving to make everything perfect and obsessing over minor issues, you will find it challenging to maintain your enthusiasm after the initial buzz has died.

Let's face it, life will throw you some curveballs along the way, and if you've made things too complex and confusing for yourself, it'll be much more challenging to keep going when things got tough.

Take, for example, if you want to lose weight and get fitter; instead of being all scientific and trying to figure out the best workout and monitoring every single calorie in your meal plan, simply put on your running shoes and go for a jog.

Many people cannot stick to their health plans because exercising has a negative connotation in their minds.

As you continue, you can add more details and level things up. But first and foremost, develop the habit of getting things started.

Efficiency is the best option. CREATIVITY vs. EFFICIENCY (where needed)

Creativity, when used correctly, is a requirement and has its place.

However, excessive inventiveness can disrupt the efficiency and flow of things, making it difficult to maintain over time.

Don't squander your creative energy on minor matters, especially when you're first starting. In everyday jobs, choose flow and efficiency, so you don't have to waste mental energy on the minor details.

Save your mental energy and ingenuity for items that will make a meaningful difference in your growth.

**Here are a couple of such examples:**

Instead of trying out different exercises every day and tiring yourself trying to figure out which ones are best for you, stick to a few fundamental, core activities and be consistent with them if you've just started exercising.

If you're beginning a business, instead of focusing all of your creative energy on producing the most advanced and elegant website possible or making your office a perfect representation of your brand, concentrate your efforts on the items or services you'll be offering.

In the long run, it is what counts most. Simply put up a primary office or website to get things started.

**Avoid "Analysis Paralysis"**

Many of us get caught up in all the intricacies and analytics because there is SO MUCH information out there. While you over-analyze things, especially when they are still in the early stages and not yielding many results, you will become frustrated and finally give up.

If you've only recently started working out and see your progress every day in the mirror or on the scale, you'll quickly become disheartened.

You won't see what you're searching for if you've recently established a business and are focusing too much on sales metrics.

Simply gather enough knowledge to develop a strong strategy, and then concentrate all of your efforts on executing it. Don't be concerned if you don't see results straight away. Things move at their own pace.

Stop obsessing on details. You'll have more peace of mind and be able to focus on giving it your all, which will help you advance more quickly in the long run.

Negative ideas and doubts should not be believed. There will be occasions when you doubt yourself or the task's ability to be completed.

**Make Goals and Expectations That Are Realistic**

"Most people overestimate their ability to do in a year and underestimate their ability to accomplish in a decade."

Many people expect results too soon after seeing other people's overnight success stories. They overestimate what they can do in six to twelve months.

It takes time for things to come together. The success tales we hear about people who become famous overnight are outliers, not the norm.

Aim for the stars, but keep your ambitions and expectations in check.

Aim for the stars, but be prepared to put in a lot of time and effort to build a rocket. Sow a seed today, and in 10 years, you'll have a fully established towering, delectable tree.

**To Avoid Burnout, Maintain a Healthy Pace.**

The initial excitement of something can lead us to overwork ourselves to the point of burnout. It's best to see this ahead of time and prevent it.

Work hard, but remember to keep a good pace and take breaks to breathe, enjoy, and relax. To freshen your mind and spirits, change things up a little.

*Consider the difference between a marathon runner and a sprinter.*

A sprinter may run extremely fast for a short period. On the other hand, the marathon runner paces himself to avoid weariness and can run for hours and hours while having fun.

"If you put a pail of water on a rock, nothing happens.

Every time you let a drop of a waterfall on a rock, it makes a hole in that rock."

– **Unidentified**

Taking a good pause and allowing yourself to unwind and rest is an essential part of pacing yourself. Even if it's only for a weekend, go on a short vacation.

When you return to work and your daily routine, you'll feel revitalized, invigorated, and ready to take on new tasks.

You take a sabbatical, confident that this relaxing time will enhance your job and progress.

In the end, no matter how much your brain tells you that you need to work all the time, you don't have to.

**VALUE AND PROGRESS IS MORE IMPORTANT THAN PERFECTION**

If there is such a thing as perfection in the human world, it can take a long time to achieve it.

When we begin something with zeal, our inner perfectionists and critics emerge to point out all flaws and errors.

All we have to do in this situation is tell that inner perfectionist and critic to STOP TALKING AND SIT HIS BUM DOWN!

Things don't always have to run flawlessly and according to plan. It's OK to make mistakes, and it's not a big issue if we make mistakes now and then.

Furthermore, the "All or Nothing" mentality is both inefficient and ineffective. We can't always give our very best. To preserve consistency, we must occasionally perform at an average level; but, this should not become a habit.

**Know When to Say No**

Being consistent necessitates the ability to say no. Because they are continually preoccupied with things that aren't necessary, it's difficult for a Yes-Man/Woman to stay consistent at something.

Prioritize your tasks and don't allow distractions to pull you away from them. If you've committed to anything, make it a top priority and say no to anything that might come in the way.

Make no commitments that you can't keep. It doesn't matter if you're making promises to yourself or others.

I've written a whole book on HOW TO SAY NO (reclaim your time, energy, and personal space). You should check it out since it will assist you with prioritizing and, as a result, staying consistent in the areas that are most important to you.

Allow yourself to forgive yourself for not being consistent, and then return to it.

Each of us is an individual with our own set of characteristics of ups and downs. There is no such thing as perfection. From time to time, you will make blunders... It is something that everyone does.

If you believe that being consistent entails never faltering, you need to rethink your definition of consistency.

It's admirable to be ambitious, but pushing yourself too hard can just make you feel bad about yourself, leading you to give up. In reality, this is counterproductive.

It's OK if you decide to run every day for the following 30 days and skip 6-7 days. That does not imply that you are unreliable.

Consider the glass to be half full. At the very least, you ran for 23-24 days, which is better than nothing!

Life gets in the way sometimes, no matter how hard we try, and that's perfectly natural. Not how well you follow through, but how quickly you get back on track if you fall off track is what determines your consistency.

Accept it and be forgiving of yourself instead of berating yourself, and then get back to work!

**Bonus tip:** Automate Your Work by Creating a System.

This last extra tip will save you months and a lot of the stress that could otherwise overwhelm you.

Whether you're looking for consistency in your personal or professional life, make it a point to create a system so that everything falls into place without you having to think about the order of things or minor details every time you do something.

You won't have to waste mental energy thinking or fret about mundane tasks after you've established a method.

Also, use programs and internet services to automate as many processes as feasible.

We live in a fortunate time when we have access to technology. Utilize technology as a servant and delegate as much work as possible to it.

Automation will significantly simplify your life, prevent you from being overwhelmed, and free up a significant how much time you have to devote to more critical jobs more critical tasks.

If you're not a techie and find the concept of automation intimidating to learn and use, I understand. I'm not a techie either, but believe me when I say it's not that difficult once you take the initiative to utilize it.

Any automated tool or service will become second nature to you in a few days, and you will be grateful that you are using it.

**Conclusion**

Analyze whatever you wish to be consistent within the light of these ten principles to determine where you've been missing out. Make it look like a to-do list.